p 29 ~ power resides in middle class; stigmatiz. of middle class

* p 52 example of God fails, Man puts it right -

Change Agents

Alinskyian Organizing Among Religious Bodies

છ

Volume I

A Brief History

By Stephanie Block

Change Agents

Alinskyian Organizing Among Religious Bodies

Volume I

A Brief History

By Stephanie Block

Spero Publishing
Published in the United States

Acknowledgements

Change Agents has been a labor of…well, not love, exactly…but passion, spanning many years. There is no way to properly acknowledge the scores of individuals who have encouraged and assisted its production.

However, I must thank my husband, Steven, who supported this work with his, despite his better judgment.

And without the indefatigable hounding of Dr. Alice von Hildebrand, the manuscript would probably have fallen into digital stillbirth.

Yet there are so many, many additional researchers, writers, and kind friends who provided resources and support. How does one begin to thank everyone? You know who you are and you're *amazing*.

Table of Contents

Acknowledgements   v

Introduction   ix

A Brief History of Faith-Based Organizing

1. A Brief History of Saul Alinsky,
   Father of Community Organizing   3

2. Target and Organize: An Introduction to
   Alinskyian Community Organizing   39

3. The Industrial Areas Foundation   61

4. ACORN: The Association of Community
   Organizations for Reform Now   75

5. PICO National Network   101

6. Gamaliel   123

7. Other Alinskyian Organizing Networks   139

8. Funding from Religious Institutions to
   Alinskyian Organizations   197

Introduction

I became aware of the Industrial Areas Foundation (IAF) in 1993, when my Albuquerque parish was targeted for membership in the IAF local being formed.

Years earlier, the pastor of the parish had been trained by the IAF and, once he took over leadership of our congregation, began the organizing process by choosing several "leaders" to participate in what he termed "a new ministry." These people were already active in the parish, well-known and respected.

It was unclear to this handpicked team what they were being asked to do. The pastor only explained the IAF was a "leadership development training program" that would enable the church to better serve the community. From that, one businesswoman understood that she was going to be taught stress reduction and time management. Another couple thought they would be learning how to interest more of the congregation in pastoral work.

The Industrial Areas Foundation sent a speaker to the parish. Again, there were more questions than answers. The leaders were told that the IAF was going to help them change the community. It would teach them to build relationships of trust and "empower" them to tackle issues and make civic decisions. The IAF would train members to analyze public life and have a voice in it. It would gather various religious denominations together into an IAF local, called Albuquerque Interfaith, to tackle social evils with ecumenical persuasiveness. It would train church lay leaders, through the use of a highly paid, professional organizer, to use their collective "power" and become politically involved.

What these changes were, *precisely*, or *how* they were to be made, was not explained. The fact that people of faith were doing the work, the speaker said, would spiritualize the work and, in turn, spiritually renew the parish itself. Some understood this to mean that Albuquerque Interfaith was going to work at putting in stoplights and improving the school system. Others wondered – aloud – if there weren't a larger social movement being proposed.

One participant requested more information and was given a list of recommended reading that included the seminal treatise, *Rules for Radicals*, written by the IAF's founder, Saul Alinsky.

This was new territory for her but she dutifully purchased the book. It repelled her. Its "dedication" to Lucifer, its unabashed aggravation of class hostilities, and its arguments against fundamental ethical principles were horrifying. As she shared various troubling passages from its pages with other parishioners, there were protests to both Father and to the Archbishop.

Questions were greeted by intense resentment and vilification of the questioners. Parishioners were told that membership in Albuquerque Interfaith was not *their* decision to make. Although the Archdiocese arranged for a mediation process between concerned parishioners and the pastor, the pastor refused to attend.

As one who was in the midst of this terribly unsettling experience, I found my curiosity peaked by the ferocity of the organizers to any opposition and by the determination of our pastor to force membership on the parish. People who had led ministries for years – the music director, the head of the parish respect life committee, the evangelization team, one deacon, members of the baptism preparation team and the parish marriage enrichment program, the head of the RCIA program, among others – were told that their "negativity" made them unfit for such service and were dismissed from service.

In researching this, it became apparent that our experience was no anomaly but a common pattern for new Alinskyian organizations.

After writing several articles on the subject, the Wanderer Forum Foundation approached me in 1996 to prepare a commentary about the IAF's primary Catholic grant source, the Campaign for Human Development (CHD). Extensive source material (exhibits), arranged in 4" ring binders, accompanied the commentary and was mailed to every ordinary in the United States in 1997. A second commentary was prepared a year later, also mailed to all the United States bishops, specifically focused in the IAF.

In the year following dissemination of the commentary, the annual appeal changed its name from Campaign for Human Development to *Catholic* Campaign for Human Development (CCHD) and, more substantively, improved its guidelines for awarding grants. Prior to these changes, CHD guidelines had simply disbarred any organization from funding whose proposed project was opposed to the Church's moral teachings. The new guidelines emphasized the sanctity of human life and stated clearly that not only must (C)CHD funded *projects* conform to the moral teachings of the Catholic Church but that any *organization* whose primary or substantial thrust was contrary to Catholic teaching – even if the project itself was in accord – would be denied funding. This was an important and critical advance.

However, actual changes in the CCHD's funding patterns were negligible. Specifically, Alinskyian organizations, despite the numerous ways they theoretically and practically contradict Church teaching, continued to receive a large percentage of CCHD grant money and, more significantly, continued to expand their presence and their anti-Catholic ideas in parishes across the country.

It is clear that while the bishops have understood, abstractly, the problem inherent to funding organizations whose work undermines Church teaching, it is also clear that they do not yet understand that Alinskyian organizing and its various locals are among them. In their anxiety to address various social problems, they are disposed to hope Alinskyian organizing may provide a solution, despite its negative elements.

It's a Faustian bargain.

A Brief History
of
Faith-Based Organizing

1. A Brief History of Saul Alinsky, Father of Community Organizing

Saul Alinsky was educated at the University of Chicago, doing graduate work in criminology where he discovered a passion for organizing, first with the Committee for Industrial Organization (CIO) and later as an independent organizer.

What made Alinsky's organizing style unique was that it brought religious bodies into its embrace. His success in collaborating with clergy came from two sources: a hearty, pragmatic approach to problem solving and an idealism that is similar to Christianity in its concern for the poor. In other respects, however, Alinskyism and Christianity are diametrically opposed.

BACK OF THE YARDS

An Alinskyian axiom is that, given a sufficiently adversarial, mutual circumstance, any two groups will become allies. Alinsky proved the point with his first major organizing effort in the Chicago slums of the late thirties. There, with the help of Bishop Bernard Sheil, a senior auxiliary bishop in the Diocese of Chicago, who was known nationally for his support of the labor movements, Alinsky brought Polish Catholics to work with Lithuanian, Slovak, German, and Irish parishes, which often brought centuries' old hatreds into the new world.[1] More strikingly, he

---

[1] Sanford D. Horwitt, *Let Them Call Me Rebel,* (New York: Vintage Books, 1989), p 70-71. The first executive board for the Back of the Yards Neighborhood Council consisted of "four priests, one each from a Polish, Lithuanian, Slovak, and Irish parish; four men and a women from church-related clubs, including

brought members of the Catholic Church — a Church that had been brutalized by Communism throughout the world and is at utter, philosophical variance with Communism's atheistic humanism — to work alongside of labor leaders, some of whom were openly Communists. Their common impulse toward a community both wished to help, brought the Church, labor leaders, and the occasional Communist organizer, into a temporary truce.

Alinsky brought these disparate factions together as the Back of the Yards Neighborhood Council, a collaboration that possessed enough collective influence to win major concessions from the recalcitrant meatpacking company that owned the Chicago stockyards and was responsible for the neighborhood's livelihood, as well as for many aspects of its wretchedness.

What Alinsky had to offer the Back of the Yards was an analysis of mutual interests. Guiding all concerned parties to discover their points of commonality, he was able to persuade each that its self-interest lay in cooperation and collective action.

To conceptualize this principle, or anti-principle, one might consider a hypothetical case in which the Methodists and the Jews of a town, who will never agree about theology, want a new public school. Their common problem is to convince the local government to make appropriations for the project. The local government's self-interest is re-election. If an organized "force" of citizens — a Jewish/Methodist coalition in this scenario — can persuade the local government that they represent a sufficiently large

---

one of the German Catholic church; three businessmen; the leader of an athletic club; a man from the Packingtown Youth Committee; the local police captain; and Herb March of the PWOC [Packinghouse Workers' Organizing Crusade - March was an organizer for the Committee for Industrial Organization and an avowed communist, ed.]." See pp 59-60.

constituency of voters, the school will be built, as it is in the "self-interest" of all parties.

In American society, comprised of a great number of different factions, such pragmatic couplings are almost taken for granted. Alinsky observed that the worldly mechanism for "change" – "change," that is, toward any desired goal that requires a political effort to achieve – comes from two sources: money and numbers. Money can be a problem for organizations that work among the poor but, when factions can be persuaded to work together, the power of numbers – people power – is quite attainable.

For example, if our fictitious town had one wealthy Methodist who was willing to build the school single-handedly, the need to petition or strong-arm local government could be circumvented altogether. That would demonstrate the power of money.

However, if the well-to-do Methodist were of a parochial mind, intending the school to be used solely for the benefit of other Methodists, the Jewish population would be left not only without a school for *its* children but also with little influence. No longer is the entire town clamoring for new facilities, but only a less "significant" minority.

Alinsky's genius was the ability to demonstrate, graphically and dramatically, a way to work for and with the "minority." The ability to say, "We represent a large group of voters" or perhaps "We represent a large group of people who will fight you," is a persuasive position from which to commence negotiations. The poor, Alinsky reasoned, are without the resource of money, but where numbers of people can be brought into a collective action, they will nevertheless be "powerful."

This "vision" carries some rather substantial problems but the Chicago Back of the Yards Neighborhood Council of the 1930s and early 40s, through the power of its collective activity, succeeded in getting garbage pick-up, street repairs, increased policing, a neighborhood health clinic and a credit union, a school hot-lunch program, and, among other things, community involvement in the lives of young criminals that significantly reduced the juvenile crime rate of the area.[2]

These were important and attractive victories. As people from other struggling communities observed the improvements acquired by the Back of the Yards, they wanted Alinsky's organizational expertise, too. To address this, Bishop Sheil suggested the establishment of a non-profit foundation to midwife community organizations around the country. He introduced Alinsky to the wealthy philanthropist Marshall Field III, who supplied the new Industrial Areas Foundation (IAF) with a $15,000 grant for Alinsky's salary and expenses. Alinsky, Sheil, and Field set up a board of trustees and the IAF was launched.[3] In the ensuing years, Field and Bishop Sheil each gave the Foundation up to $5,000 yearly and other contributors were added to the board later.

---

[2] P. David Finks, *The Radical Vision of Saul Alinsky*, (New York: Paulist Press, 1984), pp 21-22.

[3] *Let Them Call Me...*, p 103, identifies the board members as Howland Shaw (chief of foreign personnel at the US State Department and also on the board of directors for the National Conference of Catholic Charities, under Monsignor John O'Grady), Katheryn Lewis (daughter of CIO union president, John Lewis), Marshall Field III, Bishop Bernard Sheil, Saul Alinsky, Hermon Dunlop Smith (a "progressive" Republican), Britton Budd (president of the Public Service Company of Northern Illinois), Stuyvesant Peabody (of Peabody Coal Company family), and Judge Theodore Rosen (from Philadelphia).

ALINSKY AND MARITAIN

Alinsky had many Catholic friends, the most improbable ~~new also~~ of them being the philosopher Jacques Maritain.

In those early days of organizing, Saul Alinsky expressed strong opinions about the Catholic Church. There were very few leaders among the clergy, Alinsky told an audience in 1942, at the *National Conference for Catholic Charities,*

> ...who are completely committed to
> rendering their services, their abilities, and
> their lives for the benefit of their fellow
> man...[T]he teaching of Christ and the
> philosophy represented by him...is one of
> the most revolutionary documents the
> world has ever witnessed, a doctrine so
> radical that both by itself as well as in its
> implications it would make the most left-
> wing aspect of communism appear
> conservative. This radical, revolutionary
> philosophy of Catholicism makes it
> impossible for one to subscribe to it and
> yet be a centrist or a right-wing
> conservative. [Those] who have may be
> Catholics in name, but they are pagan in
> soul.[4]

[margin note: A. redefines Catholicism]

Alinsky was, of course, more correct about the radical, revolutionary nature of Catholicism than he understood.

---

[4] *Let Them Call Me...*, p 133, quoting from speech among Alinsky's papers at the University of Illinois at Chicago, 28 September 1942.

However, Alinsky, the agnostic, failed to grasp that those radical "implications" of the Church render not only right-wing, conservative politics "pagan," in so far as they operate according to the world's laws of "power," but the left-wing as well. As Alinsky knew nothing other than the vehicle of politics to achieve "change" — as that was his only "tool" for helping those who needed help — Alinsky worked within that limitation. He was determined to redress poverty using "left-wing" politics, which fomented revolution and changed governments. The Church, from his perspective, could become a tremendous force for acquiring this "common good" by contributing bodies — people power — for left-wing causes.

One isn't surprised to read that Alinsky thought this way. He observed no religious tradition and had been raised in a broken Jewish home. It is extremely surprising, however, that Alinsky's dear friend, the gentle and influential Catholic philosopher Jacques Maritain, didn't catch — or, at least, failed to address — the numerous errors in Alinsky's articulations. Maritain even went so far as to encourage Alinsky to write his first book, *Reveille for Radicals.*[5]

Maritain was too dazzled by the organization he had seen in the Back of the Yards, where ethnic rivalries gave way to fraternal good will and common effort, to be critical of Alinsky's methods — and more importantly, of his

---

[5.] *The Philosopher and the Provocateur: the Correspondence of Jacques Maritain and Saul Alinsky,* ed. with Introduction and Notes by Bernard Doering, (Notre Dame: University of Notre Dame Press, 1994), Letter of Alinsky to Maritain, July 20, 1945 "I informed the University Press in no uncertain terms that I began to write this book at your personal request..." and again on August 21, 1945 "Concerning French and Italian rights [for the translation of 'Reveille...', ed.] I have informed the press (in no uncertain terms) that I wrote this book primarily at your suggestion and urging."

ideological foundation. Maritain was too hopeful that here, at last, he might find concrete systems for actualizing Christian idealism, the "kingdom of heaven" on earth. Consequently, he was blinded to the flaws in his friend's reasoning.[6]

> …as I write these lines, I see in the Western World no more than three revolutionaries worthy of the name - Eduardo Frei in Chile, Saul Alinsky in America …and myself in France, who are not worth beans, since my call as a philosopher has obliterated my possibilities as an agitator…." [7]

But Alinsky was no Christian. While *Reveille for Radicals* was a call to action at the service of the downtrodden, Alinsky the Radical picked among mankind, himself separating the wheat from the chaff. Alinsky claimed belief

---

[6.] Hamish Fraser suggests some philosophical reasons why Maritain might have been prone to this blindness towards Alinsky in "Jacques Maritain and Saul David Alinsky: Fathers of the 'Christian' Revolution," a monograph published in Scotland, undated, pp 44-47. Maritain, says Hamish, abandoned the doctrine of Christ's social kingship – that subjects all men and therefore all societies to Christian norms – for his own concept of "integral humanism," a notion of inherent fraternal equality among all men, regardless of their beliefs. Furthermore, Maritain saw the revolutionary movements of the past as positive forces in human development.

[7] Jacques Maritain, *The Peasant of the Garonn: an old layman questions himself about the present time*, Holt Rinehart, 1968, p 23. In a footnote, he adds: "Saul Alinsky, who is a great friend of mine, is a courageous and admirably staunch organizer of people's communities…whose methods are as effective as they are unorthodox."

in the worth of the individual and in the willingness to share, personally, the pain, injustices, and sufferings of one's fellow man but condemned the individual who was not collectively unified to the "masses" to unspeakable contempt and depersonalization. One may be counted as "of the people" only if he is in agreement with the Radical. Alinsky decried raw materialism and greed but, in point of fact, worked for little else.

Reveille for Radicals taught that the "salvation of the masses will be found in the people themselves and nowhere else," and that, "we know to date most of our pain, frustration, defeat, and failure has come from using an imperfect instrument, a partial democracy."

Alinsky's Radical believed "in that brave saying by a brave people, 'Better to die on your feet than to live on your knees!'"

His Radical hated those whom he attacked "...not as persons but as symbols representing ideas or interests which he believes inimical to the welfare of the people." "Radicals precipitate the social crisis by action," "...radicals rebel...," "[the radical] will realize that in the initial stages of organization, he must deal with the qualities of ambition and self-interest as realities. Only a fool would step into a community dominated by materialistic standards and self-interest and begin to preach ideals."[8]

Never mind the multitudes of holy men and women who were just such fools, preaching just such "idealism," and who radically succeeded in altering the world around them. Never mind that the "Christian philosophy" whose adherents also share, personally, in the pain, injustices and sufferings of others, accomplishes its work with the cross of Christ.

---

[8] Saul Alinsky, *Reveille for Radicals*, (New York: Vintage Books, 1946), pp 18, 22, 92.

Alinsky's Radical insists that liberals "fail to recognize that through the achievement and constructive use of power can people better themselves. They talk glibly of people lifting themselves up by their own bootstraps but fail to realize that nothing can be lifted or moved except through power."[9]

The "vision" expressed in *Reveille for Radicals* was unabashedly political. The partisanship of parties, Republican or Democrat, was not at issue. Rather, what mattered was the political direction in which an entire people must be pushed. Eschewing capitalism, the book proclaimed that radicals:

> …hope for a future where the means of economic production will be owned by all the people instead of just a comparative handful. They feel this minority control of production facilities is injurious to the large masses of people not only because of economic monopolies but because of the political power inherent in this form of centralized economy does not augur for an ever expanding democratic way of life. [10]

This "unspecified American brand of socialism," to use the words of Alinsky biographer, Sanford Horwitt,[11] was to be accomplished through the "…democratic organization of our people for democracy. It is the job of building People's Organizations."[12]

[9.] *Reveille for Radicals*, p 22..

[10.] *Reveille for Radicals*, p 25-26.

[11.] *Let Them Call Me…*, p 172.

[12.] *Let Them Call Me…*, p 172, quoting *Reveille for Radicals*.

Again, the question is not why Alinsky came to the conclusions he did, but why certain members of the Catholic Church, and later religious institutions of all brands, responded so enthusiastically to Alinsky's thought.

Bishop Sheil was quoted in *Time Magazine* as saying that "*Reveille for Radicals* is a life-saving handbook for the salvation of democracy." Alinsky chortles in a letter to Maritain, "Incidentally, the reviews in the Catholic Press have been phenomenal. I have been completely amazed by the praise that has come from most of the Catholic papers in the country." [13]

Maritain himself, in a review for the *Chicago Tribune* wrote that in Alinsky's People's Organizations "...our great problems — how real leaders can emerge from and be chosen by real people — [are] to be solved..."

The review ended with, "I do appreciate and admire the constructive value and universal import of the essential concepts [*Reveille for Radicals*] proposes, and the new possibilities it discovers for that 'orderly revolution' which Mrs. Agnes E. Meyer[14] anticipated in describing the work started in Chicago's Packingtown."

Maritain's personal correspondence to Alinsky concerning the book was effusive. The book...

[13.] *The Philosopher and the Provocateur...,* letter of Alinsky to Maritain, May 2, 1946.

[14.] Mrs. Agnes Meyer was the wife of the publisher of the *Washington Post* and the daughter of a Lutheran minister who had little positive to say about the "authoritarianism" of the Roman Catholics. She greatly admired, however, the work of the Catholic priests she had observed in the *Back of the Yards* and had written a series of articles for the *Post* about the 'orderly revolution' of Saul Alinsky in Chicago. Maritain had been sent copies of these articles from Alinsky and wrote back that "Mrs. Eugene Meyer's Orderly Revolution is excellent. I shall try to have it reprinted in some French magazine." See *Let Them Call Me Rebel*, p 178-179 and *The Philosopher...*, p 9, 12. The term "orderly revolution" is taken out of *Reveille for Radicals,* p 198.

… reveals a new way for **real** democracy,
the only way a man's thirst for social
communion can develop and be satisfied,
through freedom and not through
totalitarianism in our disintegrated times.
You seem at first glance over optimistic, in
reality your method starting with self-
interest and egoistic concerns in order to
transform them shows how sound is your
knowledge of human nature. Your
optimism is Christ's optimism. You are a
Thomist, dear Saul, a practical Thomist![15]

THE COLD WAR WITHOUT AND WITHIN

The years following publication of *Reveille for Radicals*
were difficult ones for those on the "left." Joe McCarthy
and his supporters labored not only to purge the American
government from dangers of the "Red Menace" within, but
also conducted public hearings to flush out the private
opinions of citizens who ought to have been constitutionally
protected from such invasion.

Bishop Sheil, assisted by Alinsky, went on the offensive
after McCarthy. It was an unpopular position for the time,
particularly among Church hierarchy whose membership
contained those with first-hand experiences of Communist
atrocities. Bishop Sheil's outspokenness, coupled with a
rising concern over his fiscal mismanagement of various

[15.] *The Philosopher and the Provocateur…,* letter of Maritain to Alinsky, August
20, 1945.

projects, caused Sheil to find himself under increased and disapproving scrutiny from his superiors.

Alinsky suffered no corresponding difficulties. He was greatly admired for his organizational work in the Back of the Yards by Chicago's Cardinal Stritch and the progressively-minded Monsignor John O'Grady, founder and director of the National Conference of Catholic Charities. O'Grady felt that Catholic Charities was not sufficiently responsive to the destitute in the inner city and isolated rural areas. He believed that "the IAF's community organizing, with its coalition of local parishes and community, could provide the environment in which Catholic Charities could return to the streets."[16] Jacques Maritain had brought Alinsky together with a young, energetic Chicago priest, Father John Egan, who had became something of a "disciple" of Alinsky's. These contacts and friendships led to new organizational projects. So while Alinsky continued to move comfortably in Catholic circles, Bishop Sheil felt ostracized and unsupported, and by 1954 had broken with Alinsky altogether.

One connection led to another for Alinsky. Father Egan introduced him to a group of young Catholic intellectuals, some Marxist, some anticlerical, but all liberal. Among that group was Nicholas von Hoffman, today a columnist for the *Washington Post* and a prominent writer, but at that time a longhaired "artist" struggling with writing a novel and working as a community activist among the Puerto Rican neighborhoods of Chicago.

Alinsky, supported financially by Cardinal Stritch,[17]

[16.] *Radical Vision of Saul Alinsky,* p 75.

[17.] *Let Them Call Me…*, p 77: "Stritch agreed to contribute $4,000 to the Industrial Areas Foundation; this was the first time it received money from the archdiocese (it was, in effect, money for von Hoffman's salary)…" Previously, the IAF had been receiving "Catholic" money only from Bishop

hired Von Hoffman to prepare a detailed study of Chicago's Puerto Rican section, that would in time lead to a community organization there. Meanwhile, Alinsky had irons in other fires. Networked with influential and moneyed people in New York and around the country, for the next two decades Alinsky experimented with his "People's Organizations." When racial frustrations peaked during the sixties, Alinsky's organizations were perceived by the Church as a tool for channeling more volatile tendencies of "Black Power" into a constructive, civic action.

The experiments had flaws, even by Alinsky's standards. Back of the Yards, which had succeeded in bringing together ethnic factions for common civic endeavor, now mobilized against allowing blacks to move into the neighborhood. While Alinsky organized parallel Chicago neighborhoods to challenge the segregationist positions of the "whites," and at least one of those is still functioning today, the fact remains that Chicago was not only as resistant to neighborhood integration in the 1990s as in the 1960s, but that inner city conditions are worse today than then.

Similarly, in 1955 Msgr. O'Grady found it necessary to pull Catholic Charities support from another Alinskyian organization in St. Louis due to the discovery that it had been operating toward segregationist ends.[18] It was far from Alinsky's intention that his Back of the Yards organization or that St. Louis organization would use their civic savvy for such unethical purposes. However, here was living contradiction of Alinsky's utopian optimism that "the people" would choose to do right most of the time, if only

---

Sheil's resources.
[18] *Radical Vision of Saul Alinsky*, pp 78-82.

given the civic "tools" to do it. Alinsky and his supporters handled such contradiction in a very "human" way - they dismissed it as an anomaly.[19]

Another highly acclaimed Alinskyian "success" from those times, FIGHT, based in Rochester, New York, was famous for pushing Eastman Kodak to allot a certain proportion of its opening positions to minorities. The organization flared brightly for a few years, supported apparently even by Archbishop Fulton Sheen, who appointed one of FIGHT's members, David Finks[20] to the office of Vicar of the Poor. Without Alinsky running the show, however, FIGHT collapsed within a few years, due to internal power struggles and a lack of continued, common direction. Truly grassroots Rochester organizations, such as the ABC (Action to a Better Community) and the Urban League — those begun by the locals themselves — watched the Alinsky train pull into town, sop up resources for awhile, get a great deal of publicity for it and then pull out, leaving them to continue, far less dramatically but far more effectively, addressing the needs of neighborhood people.

Despite a general, social idealism that Alinsky shared with many Christians and with Catholics in particular, there were serious difficulties that people of faith faced in the moral swash-buckling of the Alinsky organizations. On one level, Alinsky couldn't care less what the churches thought of him; on another, he struggled to find ways to expand the laity's acceptance and support of his organizational activity.

An egregious example of the IAF's efforts to draw the faithful occurred while organizing the diocese of Cardinal

---

[19.] Later organizers are less naïve and maintain tight control over their organizations.

[20] Author of *The Radical Vision of Saul Alinsky,* and a functioning priest at the time.

Spellman (who Alinsky regarded as a "fascist" because of his uncompromising intolerance of socialist ideas[21]), in a Puerto Rican community of New York City. To Alinsky's despair, there were no pre-existing groups among the New York Puerto Ricans on which to build his community organization – a critical shortcoming because the IAF is designed to be "an organization of organizations," having discovered from bitter experience that recruiting individual membership into the IAF was too time-consuming and ineffective for its purposes.[22] So, Alinsky enlisted the cooperation of a priest and created the "Knights of Santiago," a quasi-religious fraternity.[23] Pastoral justifications were given for the group, but the organizers themselves knew that its function was social and civic action.

This was not the first time the Puerto Ricans had their spiritual sensibilities exploited by the activists. Nicholas Von Hoffman and Lester Hunt, before coming under Saul Alinsky's wing, were "inventing" Puerto Rican cultural symbols – a national tree, a national flower – and all sorts of "customs." For public relations purposes, they once arranged for six little girls in their communion dresses, leading a lamb, to pose with the mayor of Chicago.[24] The establishment of a "Knights of Santiago" in New York was, to them, just more of the same creation of elements around

---

[21.] *Let Them Call Me…*, p 249, quoting a 1953 letter by Alinsky to Agnes Meyer.

[22.] Alinsky attempted to build an organization by individual membership one time, in Syracuse, NY.

[23.] *Let Them Call Me…*, p 298, a memo and a letter from Lester Hunt, organizer for the IAF in Chelsea, NY, written in 1957 and 1958 respectively, discussing the rationale for establishing the "Knights of Santiago."

[24.] *Let Them Call Me…*, p 273, from an interview with Louis Silverman, 1983.

which they could organize.

Meanwhile, Maritain sought to promote Alinsky's work in whatever ways he could, overseeing the translation of *Reveille for Radicals* in France and Italy and, in 1958, arranging for Alinsky to fly to Milan to consult with Archbishop Montini, who became Pope Paul VI in 1963. Montini was looking for organizational expertise to counter the organizing of the Italian Communist Party. Maritain, a respected friend, had given Montini nothing but glowing reports of Alinsky's work in the United States.

> In 1958, when Maritain's friend Cardinal Montini, archbishop of Milan and later Pope Paul VI, became painfully aware that the church was losing the workers of Milan to the Communist labor unions, Maritain advised him to consult Saul Alinsky on methods of community organization and the training of leaders, and Montini brought Alinsky to Milan to do so.[25]

Alinsky was hardly the fellow to counter the Communists, however. In the evenings, after he and Montini had been discussing Montini's political concerns, Alinsky was at a local tavern with a "beautiful, gray-eyed, blonde Milanese Communist union official with whom [he] explored common interests bridging Communism and capitalism."[26] Not surprisingly, the "Rome Project" never

---

[25] Bernard Doering, "Maritain and America — Friendships," in *Understanding Maritain.* ed. Deal W. Hudson and Mathew J. Mancini (Macon, GA: Mercer University Press, 1987)

[26] *The Radical Vision of Saul Alinsky,* p 114, taken from Marion Sanders *The*

developed.

When Alinsky returned to Italy in 1960, hoping to establish an IAF European "front," he found to his tremendous disappointment that the Vatican was "right-wing," writing to his wife that "we exchange ideas as though we came from different planets."[27]

One other significant juncture between the IAF and the Catholic Church toward addressing civil rights issues found its expression in the person of Cesar Chavez. Chavez had begun organizing with Fred Ross in 1954, starting on the IAF payroll for $35 a week and helping to build up Community Service Organizations (CSO) all over California. The CSOs these two men established attacked discrimination, conducted citizenship classes and massive voter registration drives. The first woman IAF organizer, Dolores Huerta, worked on their staff.

The citizenship classes, called by the Community Service Organizations "educationals," deserve a bit of attention. Alinsky and his organizers understood that power alone was insufficient to affect social change. They felt that in civic education one might find an essential component of citizen development which would enable them to participate in self-governing. Alinsky had quoted Thomas Jefferson, "Enlighten the people generally and tyranny and oppression of body and mind will vanish like spirits at the dawn of day" as evidence that his "popular education" programs were as American as apple pie. [28]

The "educationals" CSO organizer Fred Ross conducted

Professional Radical: Conversations with Saul Alinsky, 1970, p 9.

[27] *The Radical Vision of Saul Alinsky*, pp 118-119, quoting a letter from Alinsky to Jean Graham Alinsky, April 19, 1960.

[28] *Reveille for Radicals*, chapter 9 on Popular Education, p 155.

in California consisted primarily of discussions on a given topic and a "Socratic" approach of questioning designed to pull information and conclusions from the participants. He and Alinsky found these discussion groups to be intensely stimulating, inspiring people to examine complex issues at a high level of sophistication. He felt they also invigorated the organization from within, challenging its leadership to be continually self-critical.

In 1962, Chavez and Huerta, joined later by Ross, left the IAF and began the AFL-CIO United Farm Workers union, well remembered for the 1965 grape workers strike and national boycott of grapes. The Community Service Organization saw its identity as civic, whereas Chavez and Huerta envisioned a far more militant and focused effort. In addition, Chavez drew from his roots in a manner Alinsky could not. Organizing among the predominantly Catholic Mexican-Americans, Chavez did not use religion to promote the organization. Rather he, as a Catholic, turned to religion to find inner strength. His discipline of prayer and fasting led one IAF-sympathetic journalist to complain, "Today Cesar Chavez meditates in the mountains while the UFW hemorrhages."[29]

Alinsky's "style" was also at odds with the young, romantic members of the "New Left," Students for a Democratic Society, such as Tom Hayden and Paul Booth. The young activists lived in the ghetto, surviving on a strict food budget that they hoped gave them an understanding for the struggles of the poor. Alinsky thought them naive and unpractical. They were proponents of "participatory democracy," too, which consisted of town hall meetings and consensus building. Alinsky's IAF approached its

---

[29.] Kaye Northcott, "To Agitate the Dispossessed...On the Road with Ernie Cortes," *Southern Exposure*, July/August 1985.

"democracy"-building differently, dependent on the development of a like-minded leadership, philosophically aimed at creating a citizen-based, representative democracy from the leadership, down.[30]

The differences were no hindrance to collaboration, however. Alinsky brought a Hayden comrade, Staughton Lynd, to teach for a year at his training institute in Chicago. And in 1969, Paul Booth was chairing an Alinsky action, the Campaign against Pollution, also in Chicago. These were part of the pragmatic "compromises" a political activist makes.

By 1968, Alinsky's popularity was matched by his notoriety. He was trying to build an IAF training institute, but within each IAF-supporting denomination, church-goers were divided, conducting "internal debates over Alinsky's intentions and methods and over the role the churches should be playing in political affairs."[31] In addition, those who were concerned that the IAF was inherently socialist, or who, like its own Back of the Yards, opposed IAF goals of racial integration,[32] resented church funds being used to build the organization. In order to filter money less visibly, and therefore less controversially, into the IAF, the national Interreligious Foundation for Community Organizations was established to be an "ecumenical front" which would "shield the churches supporting community organizations from the growing

---

[30] *Let Them Call Me...*, pp 524-525.

[31] *The Radical Vision of Saul Alinsky*, p 167.

[32] The irony, here, is that while the IAF and those who supported its work gave lip service to racial integration, early Alinskyian community organizations pushed black empowerment.

anti-Alinsky" sentiments of their congregations.[33]
Contributions were collected by the local churches for
programs addressing racial issues and then given to the
Interreligious Foundation for Community Organizations to
distribute appropriately. Ironically, and from the IAF
perspective, infuriatingly, the whole scheme backfired
when the IFCO leadership decided that the money should
go into black-led organizing.

An alternative funding mechanism was needed if the IAF
training institute and its various local organizing projects
were to succeed. A small group of Catholic churchmen
(including Msgr. Jack Egan and then-Father David Finks,
two IAF organizers), meeting in Combermere, Canada,
conceived of a new "charity," which would become the
Campaign for Human Development.[34] The collection was
sold as a "Crusade against Poverty" and similar slogans were
used to raise millions of dollars from generous Catholics
each year.[35]

However, the mechanism by which poverty was to be
tackled was quite novel. The Campaign for Human
Development's founding resolution read:

> There is an evident need for funds
> designated to be used for organizing
> groups of white and minority poor to
> develop economic and political power in
> their own communities...therefore be it
> resolved that the National Conference of
> Catholic Bishops establish a National

---

[33] *The Radical Vision of Saul Alinsky*, p 234.
[34] Now called the *Catholic* Campaign for Human Development.
[35] "For God's Sake: Dare to break the hellish circle of poverty" is another
one of many slogans that CHD has used over the past 25 years.

Crusade Against Poverty. The Crusade
will commit the Church to raise a fund of
50 million dollars over the next several
years.[36]

The Campaign was never *intended* as an anti-poverty
program, *per se,* but was created to support community
organizing – Alinskyian community organizing. Sanford
Horwitt writes:

As for the Roman Catholic Church, its
commitment [to the IAF] both in principle
and funding is stronger than ever. Except
within certain religious and activist circles,
it is not widely known that the Church's
Campaign for Human Development
expends most of its $8 million annual
budget in grants to community organizing
and related grassroots empowerment
efforts. And many recipients of CHD
largess are IAF-directed projects.[37]

---

[36] "Resolution on the Crusade Against Poverty," adopted by the National
Conference of Catholic Bishops 11-14-69, as quoted in Daring to Seek
Justice, ed. James Jennings (Washington: United States Catholic Conference,
1986), p 69.

[37] *Let Them Call Me...,* p 586. Alinsky's other biographer, David Finks, also
writes: "The largest single contributor to these citizen organizations over the
last decade has been the *CHD" (The Radical Vision...,* p 271). Rael Jean and
Erich Isaac write, "The Catholic Church has also been a major contributor to
the utopians through its Campaign for Human Development...The largest
grants have gone to community-organizing projects of the Alinsky school: the
largest single recipient has been the Industrial Areas Foundation..." (*The
Coercive Utopians,* p 210). Robert Kleidman, Associate Professor for the

Finks says something similar:

> [T]he NCCB Urban Task Force, the
> Catholic Committee for Urban Ministry,
> my years on staff at USCC/NCCB, the
> organization and selling to the bishops of
> the Campaign for Human Development —
> all were an attempt to make available and
> find support for Alinsky's approach to
> community organization, empowerment
> of USA citizens from the bottom up, and
> what his IAF successors now call
> church/congregation-based organizing. As
> for me, I loved Saul. He stood me on my
> head and showed me a radically different
> way to see the world, the church, and
> democratic politics. [38]

Forty years later, it's possible to see just how much
Catholic money went toward establishing these community
organizations.

Department of Sociology, Cleveland State University, writes in "Community
Organizing: A View from the Bottom Up," 1994: "In 1969, concerned about
growing tensions between white ethnic and minority communities,
Monsignor Gino Baroni convinced the Conference [National Conference of
Catholic Bishops] to create the Catholic Campaign for Human Development
(CCHD), which soon became a major funder of community organizing
throughout the United States."

[38] Lawrence J. Engel, "The Influence of Saul Alinsky on the Campaign for
Human Development," Theological Studies, December 1998, Finks to the
author, October 28, 1994. Engel's thesis is that CHD, founded to support
Alinskyian organizing, was implemented as response to fears of racial unrest
during a socially chaotic period of US history.

Internal 1981-99 data from the
CHD…The table below breaks down by
network the totals for 1981-99 and for the
most recent year available, 1999
($3,044,000 in total 1999 disbursements
to four faith-based organizing networks).

	1981-99	1999
PICO	17.7%	23.8%
Industrial Areas Foundation	57.3%	50.4%
Gamaliel	15.%	15.1%
DART	9.5%	10.7%

The author who submits these numbers explains:

The primary funders of community
organizing over the last three decades have
been the Catholic bishops' Catholic
Campaign for Human Development and,
to a lesser extent, various Protestant
funding agencies. Essentially all federal
funding of community organizing was
eliminated in the late 1970s and early
1980s; CHD funding has been particularly
essential since that time, with
$27,917,500 having been disbursed to the
four faith-based organizing networks in

755 grants since 1981." [39]

Meanwhile, the philosophical foundation behind these organizations was becoming more public. Alinsky's second and last book, *Rules for Radicals*, was published in 1971. This time, Maritain, although full of praise, had reservations. He would not have used, perhaps, Alinsky's phrase of "self-contradiction" to describe the necessary attitude of the organizer who is facing a constantly shifting political landscape, for example, but Maritain was prepared to dismiss the unhappy choice of words as a philosophical problem that, on the "level of pure action [is] a kind of boldness…"

Nor was Maritain comfortable with Alinsky's essential assertion in *Rules…* that "the ends justify the means." Maritain rationalized, however, that Alinsky didn't quite mean what he was saying, as evidenced by how he had donated his life for the service of human dignity, and he assured Alinsky that his book would be of enormous social benefit. [40] Reading Maritain's letter, one senses the writer's discomfort with his friend's work. *Rules for Radicals,* however, contains significant philosophical mistakes that render it utterly incompatible with Christianity, as Maritain was no doubt well aware.

David Finks, another friend of Alinsky's who organized with him and wrote the biography, *The Radical Vision of Saul Alinsky*, also finds it necessary to "interpret" the *Rules*. He simply ignores the "controversial" parts. Fink and Maritain

---

[39] Richard L. Wood, *Faith in America: Religion, Race, and Democratic Organizing in America,* University of Chicago Press, 2002, p 292, FN 3. Further information about the Catholic Campaign for Human Development is in chapter 9.

[40]. *The Philosopher and the Provocateur*, letter of Maritain to Alinsky, September 19, 1971.

"know" what Alinsky *meant*. Through the eyes of friendship, they navigate the briar patch of Alinsky's ideas and acknowledge only its blossoms.

The real Alinsky, however, was a complex man. Touchingly tender and "spiritual" in his letters to Maritain, he was unabashedly profane in his organizing. A fiery moralist for social justice, his personal morals were "loose" and frequently self-serving. Egocentric and self-sacrificing in turn, an agnostic who sought out and clung to religion, Alinsky is not an easy man to understand. Therefore, those who loved him tended to drink at his genius and to wink at the rest.

Unfortunately, those who haven't Fink and Maritain's prejudice of personal attachment must study the *Rules* as they find it. Alinsky's ideas must stand on their own merit, as the organization Alinsky built will grow logically upon the foundation he constructed. The maturing plant will reveal the health of its seed.

Rules for Radicals

Rules for Radicals opens with a quote by Saul Alinsky:

> Lest we forget at least an over-the shoulder acknowledgment to the very first radical: from all our legends, mythology, and history (and who is to know where mythology leaves off and history begins—or which is which), the first radical known to man who rebelled against the establishment and did it so effectively that he at

least won his own kingdom – Lucifer. [41]

This fundamental rebelliousness is the heart of Alinsky's worldview. On one level, his revolution isn't old-fashioned communism but a generic and perpetual struggle of the lower classes to get out from under the upper class. On a deeper level, however, Alinsky wants to liberate Man from "enslavement" to dogma, for he believes "the truth is changing and relative."[42]

Alinsky wrote *Rules for Radicals* to give people the tools he sees as achieving self-liberation. "Here I propose to present an arrangement of certain facts and general concepts of change, a step toward a science of revolution."[43]

He builds on the tactical principles of Machiavelli: *"The Prince* was written by Machiavelli for the Haves on how to hold power. *Rules for Radicals* is written for the Have-Nots on how to take it away."[44]

Rules is concerned with power acquisition: "My aim here is to suggest how to organize for power: how to get it and how to use it."[45]

This is not accomplished through assistance to the poor, or even by organizing the poor to demand assistance: "…[E]ven if all the low-income parts of our population were organized…it would not be powerful enough to get significant, basic, needed changes."[46]

Those *basic changes* require the cooperation of a larger proportion of the population and Alinsky advises the

---

[41] *Rules,* dedication page.

[42] *Rules…*, p. 11.

[43] *Rules…*, p. 7.

[44] *Rules,* p 3.

[45] *Rules.,* p 10.

[46] *Rules,* p 184.

organizer to target the middle class, rather than the poor: "Organization for action will now and in the decade ahead center upon America's white middle class. That is where the power is."[47] Alinsky is interested in the middle class solely for its usefulness:

> Our rebels have contemptuously rejected the values and way of life of the middle class. They have stigmatized it as materialistic, decadent, bourgeois, degenerate, imperialistic, war-mongering, brutalized and corrupt. They are right, but we must begin from where we are if we are to build power for change, and the power and the people are in the middle class majority.[48]

The middle class, unappealing as it might be, is a valuable pawn in power plays orchestrated by the organizer. To accomplish this, Alinsky writes that the organizer must "begin to dissect and examine that way of life [the middle class lifestyle]...He will know that 'square' is no longer to be dismissed as such — instead his own approach must be 'square' enough to get the action started."[49]

Without fixed moral truth, *Rules for Radicals* avers that the end justifies the means, "The third rule of the ethics of

---

[47] *Rules*, p184.

[48] *Rules*, p 185.

[49] *Rules*, p 185-186.

means and ends is that in war the end justifies almost any means. [50]

"To say that corrupt means corrupt the ends," writes Alinsky, "is to believe in the immaculate conception of ends and principles….the practical revolutionary will understand…[that] in action, one does not always enjoy the luxury of a decision that is consistent both with one's individual conscience and the good of mankind." [51]

Altogether, Alinsky provides eleven rules of the ethics of means and ends. They are morally relativistic:

> The practical revolutionary will understand
> Goethe's 'conscience is the virtue of observers
> and not of agents of action;' in action, one does
> not always enjoy the luxury of a decision that is
> consistent both with one's individual
> conscience and the good of mankind. [52]

"The second rule of the ethics of means and ends is that the judgment of the ethics of means is dependent on the political position of those sitting in judgment." [53] Alinsky elaborates his meaning on this point, saying that if you were a member of the underground Resistance,

> …then you adopted the means of assassination,
> terror, property destruction, the bombing of
> tunnels and trains, kidnapping, and the
> willingness to sacrifice of innocent hostages to
> the end of defeating the Nazis. Those who

---

[50] *Rules*, p 29.
[51] *Rules*,, p 24-25.
[52] *Rules*, p 25.
[53] *Rules*, p 26.

opposed the Nazi conquerors regarded the
Resistance as a secret army of selfless, patriotic
idealists….To the occupation authorities,
however, these people were lawless terrorists,
murderers, saboteurs, assassins, who believed
the ends justified the means, and were utterly
unethical…[54]

Rules for Radicals is therefore only concerned with
winning. "…[I]n such a conflict, neither protagonist is
concerned with any value except victory."[55]

The winner writes the history books, as they say, "There
can be no such thing as a successful traitor, for if one
succeeds, he becomes a founding father."[56]

Cynically, Alinsky does see a use for morality and
teaches the organizer that he must give a moral
appearance, as opposed to behaving morally. "All effective
action requires the passport of morality."[57] The tenth rule
of the ethics of means and ends states "that you do what
you can with what you have and clothe it with moral
garments. ….Moral rationalization is indispensable at all
times of action whether to justify the selection or the use
of ends or means."[58]

In addition to Alinsky's highly flawed moral
foundation, he provides the organizer with a tactical style
for community organization that assumes an adversarial

---

[54] *Rules*, p 26-27.

[55] *Rules*, p 27.

[56] *Rules*, p 34.

[57] *Rules*, p 44.

[58] *Rules*, p 43.

relationship between groups of people in which one either dominates or is dominated.

-The first rule of power tactics is: power is not only what you have but what the enemy thinks you have.[59]

-Wherever possible go outside the experience of the enemy. Here you want to cause confusion, fear, and retreat.[60]

-Make the enemy live up to their own book of rules. You can kill them with this. They can no more obey their own rules than the Christian church can live up to Christianity.[61]

-Ridicule is man's most potent weapon. It is almost impossible to counterattack ridicule. Also, it infuriates the opposition, who then react to your advantage.[62]

-The threat is generally more terrifying than the thing itself.[63]

-In a fight almost anything goes. It almost reaches the point where you stop to apologize if a chance blow lands above the belt.[64]

-Pick the target, freeze it, personalize it, and polarize it.[65]

---

[59] *Rules,*, p 127.
[60] *Rules,* p 127.
[61] *Rules,* p 128.
[62] *Rules,* p 128.
[63] *Rules,* p 129.
[64] *Rules,* p 129-130.
[65] *Rules,* p 130.

- One of the criteria for picking the target is the target's vulnerability….the other important point in the choosing of a target is that it must be a personification, not something general and abstract. [66]

- The enemy properly goaded and guided in his reaction will be your major strength. [67]

This is diametrically opposed to the principles of Catholic social justice, which is the oldest, systematic body of thought on the subject. According to that reasoning, social justice is only achieved by personal virtue and within natural structures (strong families, benevolent guilds, etc.) that nurture cooperation and solidarity among all parties. A society of antagonists is hell.

Saul Alinsky also developed re-education programs. Specifically, he urged the active and deliberate "consciousness-raising" of people through the technique of "popular education." [68] Popular education is a method by which an organizer leads people to a class-based interpretation of their grievances and to accept the organizer's systemic solutions to address those grievances. [69]

---

[66] *Rules*, p 133.

[67] *Rules*, p 136.

[68] Saul Alinsky, *Reveille for Radicals*, Vintage Books, New York, 1946, 1969, chapter 9 - "Popular Education."

[69] "Popular Education" was developed by Paulo Freire who was exiled from his native Brazil for using the technique to stir Brazilian peasants to revolution. Freire came to the United States where he was highly influential.

> Through the People's Organization these groups [of citizens] discover that what they considered primarily their individual problem is also the problem of others, and furthermore the only hope for solving an issue of such titanic proportions is by pooling all their efforts and strengths. That appreciation and conclusion is an educational process.[70]

To accomplish any desired "change" requires power. "The ego of the organizer is stronger and more monumental than the ego of the leader. The leader is driven by the desire for power, while the organizer is driven by the desire to create. The organizer is in a true sense reaching for the highest level for which a man can reach — to create, to be a 'great creator,' 'to play God.'"[71]

Alinskyian organizing networks do not repudiate Saul Alinsky's organizing philosophy. The modern-day Industrial Areas Foundation, founded by Alinsky, openly acknowledges its debt and the *Rules* remains recommended reading.[72] There is a sort of "apostolic succession" among lead organizers, whose credentials either include training with Alinsky directly or with those who were themselves Alinsky-trained.[73] In 1996, when the IAF was organizing a local in Chicago, this connection to the founder was a point of authenticity. "CMS [Chicago Metropolitan Sponsors] has hired IAF to do its organizing, a coup for Monsignor John Egan, a longtime Alinsky supporter, IAF board member, and activist on Chicago

---

[70] *Reveille...* p 156. See chapter 18 for more detail on popular education.
[71] *Rules...* p. 61.
[72] IAF website: www.industrialareasfoundation.org/iafprint/iafprint.htm (accessed 3-12-09)
[73] See Appendix 1 on Alinskyian Organizing Genealogy.

urban issues."[74]

Of greater concern, however, is the recalcitrant embrace of Alinsky's amoral philosophical positions:

All participants in the Industrial Areas
Foundation national training programs are
given a reprint of a 1933 article by John H.
Randall, Jr. titled "The Importance of Being
Unprincipled."...The thesis is that because
politics is nothing but the "practical method of
compromise," only two kinds of people can
afford the luxury of acting on
principle...everyone else who wants to be
effective in politics has to learn to be
"unprincipled" enough to compromise in
order to see their principles succeed.[75]

This idea has been echoed by Ernesto Cortes, Southwest Regional Director of the IAF: "One of the worst things you can be is overly principled. Everybody has got to compromise, adapt, change. So one of the hard things we've always had to learn in the world as it is, is that there are no permanent enemies and no permanent

---

[74] Page: 35
Mary Abowd, 1996 *Neighborhood Works*,
http://www.cnt.org/tnw/19b/195sb3.htm
[75] Mary Beth Rogers, *Cold Anger: A Story of Faith and Power in Politics*,
University of North Texas Press, 1990, p 210, footnotes for chapter 16, #4.
Cold Anger was recommended reading to Catholics inquiring about more
information during the formation of Albuquerque Interfaith, an IAF affiliate
in New Mexico, in 1993. It remains suggested reading at the IAF website:
www.industrialareasfoundation.org/iafprint/iafprintaboutiaf.htm (accessed
3-12-09)

allies."[76]

This doesn't imply that the contemporary IAF has changed nothing that Alinsky put into place. It is adamant that organizers earn a competitive salary and it has certainly abandoned Alinsky's original vision of self-determination of people through local control and replaced it with a nationally networked organization. "After Alinsky died in 1972, the foundation's leadership passed to Edward T. Chambers, who believed it was necessary to create a formal national network of community organizations with stronger links between the groups."[77]

Aside from these structural changes, however, the essential and unethical principles of Saul Alinsky's organizing theory are brazenly upheld by the networks built on them.

Case Study: Alinskyian Organizing in Southern California

Saul Alinsky and California go way back. Throughout the 1940s, basking in the success of organizing efforts in the East, Alinsky looked for a way to run a project on the West Coast. After a 1947 meeting with the experienced organizer Fred Ross, in a Los Angeles hotel restaurant, Ross took a job with Alinsky's Industrial Areas Foundation.

Ross' organizational targets were Mexican-Americans. Initial issues concerned both conditions in the *barrios* — inferior schools,

---

[76] Ernesto Cortes, "Organizing the Community," *The Texas Observer,* July 11, 1986.
[77] Meg Sommerfeld, "Ordinary People," *Education Week,"* January 25, 1995, "Alinsky's Legacy," side bar.

unpaved streets, housing shortages, and so forth – and the candidacy of a young social worker, Edward R. Roybal, for the Los Angeles City Council. Roybal lost the election.

Roybal, however, did not accept defeat quietly. In an attempt to keep interest alive in his candidacy, he and his supporters formed the Community Service Organization (CSO), which had as its focus voter registration and community grievances. Ross, looking for a "hole into the community," slowly worked his way into the inner circle of CSO, visiting the homes of its leadership and both listening to their concerns and bringing out his own proposals for organizational expansion and action. Alinsky and Ross maintained fairly close contact, with Alinsky visiting Los Angeles several times a year to see for himself how the organizing was going and Ross submitting monthly reports to Alinsky.

By 1949, CSO – which was careful to avoid overt partisanship – had registered 17,000 new voters who were told that the right Los Angeles City Councilman could effectively battle discrimination problems. When Roybal was at last elected to the Council that summer, CSO received much of the credit.

During the fifties, CSO served as a training ground for young organizers, most notably César Chavez and Dolores Huerta, who went on to build the National Farm Workers Association (later called the United Farm Workers). The work of CSO itself was overshadowed by these developments, and petered out.

From its roots, however, new IAF organizing efforts blossomed. The east Los Angeles United Neighborhoods Organization (UNO) was founded in 1976 by IAF organizers, supported by priests who were familiar with the farm workers movement (including Bishop Juan Arzube). The Southern

California Organizing Committee (SCOC) was created in south-central Los Angeles in 1981. East Valley Organization (EVO) in the San Gabriel Valley was created by the IAF in 1987 and a year later Valley Organized in Community Efforts (VOICE), in the east San Fernando Valley just outside of Los Angeles. The four affiliates and their various projects were brought together in 1999 under the umbrella organization, LA Metro, to address city-wide concerns and the IAF West Coast Vision was created as a network with additional affiliates from around the state.

2. Target and Organize

An introduction to Alinskyian community organizing

There is an Alinskyian community organization in most major US cities. [78]

Yet, considering the enormous number of such organizations, few of the people they claim to represent are aware of their existence let alone that they are members. That's because most Alinskyian community organizations have an *institutional* membership – that is, they are not joined by individual people but by congregations, schools, unions, and the like. Someone attending St. Everyman's Parish or enrolled in Union for All Workers might have to read his bulletin or union newsletter very closely before learning that St. Everyman or the UAW belongs to a community organization…and, even when learning that fact, may have little idea what membership imports.

Many Alinskyian community organizations prefer institutional members, particularly those of a religious nature, because they have a pre-existing structure, access to money, and an immediate moral credibility. [79] The handbook from one Alinskyian network of community organizations explains: "[O]ne of the largest reservoirs of untapped power is the institution of the parish and congregation. Religious institutions

---

[78] The term "Alinskyian" is used to describe the organizations created along the theories and work of Saul Alinsky. For more information about Alinsky, see Chapter 2. For information about specific networks, see chapters 3-9.

[79] The notable exception to this is ACORN (the Association of Community Organizations for Reform Now), which has *individual* membership. ACORN is also an Alinskyian community organizing network, as explained in Chapter 7.

form the center of the organization. They have the people, the values, and the money."[80]

Ernesto Cortes, the Southwest Regional Director of the IAF, is quite open about the utilitarian nature of such organizational collaborations: "[T]he IAF relies on churches as a primary source of funds and troops...The churches give us stability."[81] A government report on neighborhoods, containing a case study on the IAF local of San Antonio, Texas, takes the point further still:[82]

> Often people are told by their priests in Mass to attend training sessions, actions, meetings, or to register to vote. Parishioners hear announcements from the pulpits where buses will pick them up to carry them to the tax polls [sic] to vote. Sometimes their priest leads them into action on an issue. That sense of legitimacy provided by the church is crucial.[83]

If the member institutions are primarily *religious*, the community organization is dubbed "*faith-based.*" If the member institutions are predominantly *secular*, the community organization is "*broad-based.*" Whether faith-based or broad-based, whether institution-based or individual-based, however, most Alinskyian community organizations belong to a *network* – a national body to which the locals are affiliated. The local

---

[80] Industrial Areas Foundation, *Organizing for Family and Church*, IAF publication, undated, p 18.
[81] Kay Northcott, "To Agitate the Dispossessed," *Southern Exposure*, July/August 1985.
[82] Communities Organized for Public Service (COPS)
[83] "People, Building Neighborhoods," Case Study Appendix Vol. I p 470, from the Final Report to the President and Congress of the United States prepared by the National Commission on Neighborhoods, Joseph F. Timilty, Chairman, 1979.

affiliates in each of the Alinskyian community organizing networks are bound to one another under lead organizers. They give "dues" to the national body, have their local leadership trained by the national body, and are directed by the national body to work for common goals.

"GRASSROOTS"

Therefore, the idea that Alinskyian organizations are grassroots is a romantic fiction. Early organizers sincerely taught the virtues of local governance and grassroots activism. They genuinely and quite reasonably believed that a State best serves its people at the most local level possible (subsidiarity) and that an active and engaged citizenry will best serve the common good.

Contemporary organizers, on the other hand, call themselves "grassroots" in situations where they think the term will resonate, but in practice find the problems of subsidiary governance outweigh the advantages of a large, centralized system. Similarly, an active, engaged citizenry is most useful when coordinated and directed. After all, there is no guarantee that an engaged citizenry will serve the common good – just consider the Ku Klux Klan. Nor is there any guarantee that a local government will be less corrupt or more manageable than a federal government. Worldly ideals are only as *useful* as people – both the governed and the governing – are *good*.

Furthermore, they are extremely vulnerable to manipulation. The Alinskyites have used these ideas to build community organizations that are neither grassroots nor ultimately concerned about local governance except as a tool to teach civic activism and promote federal projects.

If a community organization were *actually* grassroots, local citizens would themselves determine the need to be organized. They, themselves, would build the organization around local concerns and they, themselves, would manage it.

Alinskyian community organizations, on the other hand, are established by people from one of the national networks. The organizers decide at the national — and even international — level where they will expand. *They* identify and choose the local "leadership" of the target area. *They* train the local leadership and eventually will guide the local affiliate to support the national agenda. Lastly, the local affiliate supports the national network with dues.

The Alinskyian community organizing networks predetermine, from their top level of management, where they want a presence. For example, prior to 1992 a national organizer for the Alinskyian Industrial Areas Foundation network (IAF) said:

> Generally, our hope is that by 1996 we would be in twice the strategically located states as we are now and that would give us the capacity to develop either the regional or national base to look at national politics. If we were in the right fifteen or sixteen states, we wouldn't have to be in all fifty states. That would give us enough clout to be able to affect policies, whether it was through political parties or corporations. [84]

A 1987 master's thesis, exploring the use of rhetoric within a contemporary social movement (as evidenced by a Texas IAF local), describes something similar:

> According to one journalistic report...the IAF took an

---

[84] William Greider, *Who Will Tell the People*, 1992, pp. 235-237, quoting Arnold Graf.

'experimental tact' [sic] in the Rio Grande Valley. Rather than insisting on a local sponsoring committee for the new organization, the Texas bishops who had been funding Cortes[85] agreed to build a statewide sponsor, Texas Interfaith, comprised of IAF affiliates in San Antonio, Fort Worth, Houston, and El Paso. This group became the sponsor and provided much of the initial money for Valley Interfaith. [86]

A local IAF-trained clergyman, Rev. Johnny Youngblood, from New York, was the bluntest of all: "We are not a grassroots organization. Grass roots are shallow roots. Grass roots are fragile roots. Our roots are deep roots." [87]

This opinion is echoed by another one of the networks, PICO: "Grassroots are often unfocused and undisciplined in their work, often have trouble staying on message…The PICO California Project, however, does not share any of these weaknesses."[88]

Before moving into the targeted area, an Alinskyian network must identify a progressive leadership, called a "sponsoring committee." National organizers handpick and train this committee.

---

[85] Lead organizer of the San Antonio IAF local.

[86] Maryann Meyer Eklund, "Structure and Function of the Rhetoric of Valley Interfaith: A Case Study of a Contemporary Movement," Thesis in partial fulfillment for Master of Arts in Speech Communication, University of New Mexico, 1987.

[87] Harry Boyte, *Commonwealth: A Return to Citizen Politics*, Free Press, NY, 1990, quoting IAF leader Rev. Johnny Ray Youngblood at an IAF local (*East Brooklyn Congregations*) rally in Brooklyn.

[88] "Higher Power…," quoting Paul Speer (2002) interviews of "key informants in California state government and elite political society regarding their perceptions of the PICO California Project."

New Mexico's IAF local, Albuquerque Interfaith, was started in the early 1990s through the direct efforts of Rev. Minerva Carcaño, formerly a clerical leader in a Texas' IAF local, Valley Interfaith.[89] She began in Albuquerque by attending the meetings of several progressive local groups, including the radical Southwest Organizing Project, and there met a responsive, activist priest. These two were then able to identify several other progressive priests and ministers, sell them on the idea of forming an IAF affiliate in New Mexico, and with them form a sponsoring committee. The sponsoring committee's job was to "invite" an organizer to the city and make a financial commitment to cover the organizer's salary, benefits, office and basic expenses for the agreed period. The sponsoring – that is, preliminary – organizations are:

> …composed of representatives of churches or other religious-affiliated organizations such as charities, social service agencies, or religious orders.….[t]he sponsoring committee's job was to raise enough seed money to finance at least a two-year organizing effort, including money to pay a full-time organizer, cover office and clerical expenses, and contract…to set up leader training programs. In some cases, local sponsoring committees might enter into a "pre-organizing" contract…[90]

From where does the money come? By December 1993, the IAF sponsoring committee in Albuquerque had applied for – and been awarded – "seed money" grants through the Catholic Campaign for Human Development and several other

---

[89] Eklund, *Rhetoric* … p 50. Eklund mentions Carcaño's involvement with Valley Interfaith in Texas.

[90] Rogers, *Cold Anger*…p 178.

denominational "social justice" charities. [91] The full-time, well-paid organizer, hired from the IAF to organize in Albuquerque, came from the same Texas IAF local as Rev. Carcaño. [92]

The organizers and supporting clerics of Albuquerque Interfaith explained none of this to the congregations they were wooing. They told these congregations that the sponsoring committee, feeling the need for a community organization in the area, had researched various organizational approaches and found the IAF to be the most useful. [93] They couldn't or wouldn't say why they needed an organization and they never mentioned the years of national planning behind Albuquerque Interfaith.

Albuquerque Interfaith is an example of a faith-based organization, operating primarily through congregations. There are other models. In Washington State, largely an unchurched area, religious institutions were an ineffective target for organizing so the IAF instead approached the teacher's union, the Washington Education Association. Through the union, IAF organizers identified "progressive" principals who would be

---

[91] *1994 Albuquerque Interfaith Quarterly Report to the CHD, Policy Making Board Profile;* Archdiocesan Office of Social Justice, "CHD Plus Archdiocese Equals Mutual Growth," *People of God,* monthly publication of the Archdiocese of Santa Fe, October 1994.

[92] 1994 Albuquerque Interfaith Quarterly Report to the CHD, biography of Tim McCluskey, lead organizer for Albuquerque Interfaith, states that he was a priest serving St. Timothy's Roman Catholic Church, San Antonio, Texas from 1982-85, and was lead organizer of Valley Interfaith in 1986. McCluskey is also identified as an IAF organizer of Valley Interfaith (Texas) in "Vision, Values, Action," Texas IAF Network, undated (@ 1990)

[93] Ascension Parish Meeting with Albuquerque Interfaith organizer Tim McCluskey and IAF clerical leader Minerva Carcaño, May 31, 1994, from notes taken by author. Parenthetically, Carcaño became a United Methodist bishop in 2004.

receptive to a particular brand of education "reform."[94] IAF organizing in England took a similar approach. These are broad-based organizations.

On occasion, a local sponsoring committee may be dispensed with altogether, as was the case of the IAF's organizing in the Texas Rio Grande Valley where the IAF persuaded several Texas Catholic bishops to provide the initial support base for a regional affiliate.

Regardless of varying approaches, however, one thing is. common to all: they are not a grassroots entities.

Once a sponsoring committee is identified, the new Alinskyian organization must build the next level of "leadership" and expand its membership. The selection of this leadership is accomplished through "one on ones" – a process of private discussions with many individuals to identify those whose values are compatible with the organization, who are well connected in the community, and who are open to being recruited to work for the organization.

A select "leadership" provides the community organization with a cooperative core of people – a "leadership team." Leadership teams support the organizational platform and bring other people to organizational rallies. Individuals who fail in either of these tasks are removed from the team.

The organization *trains* its leaders. Its initial training is conducted locally and inculcates basic formational strategies. Sister Mary Beth Larkin, an experienced organizer from Texas, made several trips to New Mexico during the early 1990s, giving informational and promotional presentations to "leaders" of the new IAF affiliate, explaining the IAF's methods and teaching the principles of conducting "house-meetings."

Once a local organization is established, particularly promising leaders are invited to more intensive trainings at one

---

[94] This will be discussed in more detail in volume II of *Change Agents*.

of several centers around the country.[95]

Each leader commits to holding a certain number of *house-meetings*, usually in his or her home. House-meetings help organizers to meet the people of a neighborhood, to identify more leadership, and to discover issues of interest to the neighborhood that will also be useful to the organization. These issues must provide opportunities to train the new leaders – that is, they must be a good vehicle for organizational praxis in "civic education."

These initial issues may or may not be related to projects promoted by the national network. The point is to get a number of people from member institutions interested in and supportive of the local organization.

In other words, the meetings are not designed to let local people determine the direction of the new community organization. Rather, they assist the organizers in planning the organization's next level of activity.

CONTROLLING THE "AGENDA"

House-meetings are "guided" – that is, while attendees may discuss any issue they like, the organizer will only act on those that are useful to the organization. His goal is the development of an "educated" population that will support the larger organizational agenda.

Back in the 1980s, Msgr. Jack Egan, a Chicago IAF leader, said:

I believe that people are first interested in issues as

---

[95] This will be discussed in more detail in a subsequent volume of *Change Agents*.

they relate to their own lives. Then they can move from that dimension to citywide or statewide questions. It's a process, a widening of horizons…I believe that people can be helped to see the connections….[U]nless the local church or community begins to educate the people of the community to the international dimension of issues, they are doing a disservice.[96]

Ernesto Cortes, southwestern regional IAF director, wrote something similar: The organizer's…

…issue gets dealt with last. If you want your issue to be dealt with first, you'll never build anything. So you lead with other people's issues, and you teach them how to act on their issues. Then you model what is to be reciprocal, you model what it is to have a long-term vision.[97]

Therefore, it is the agenda of the Alinskyian lead organizers, operating as managers of the national network, who determine where the network is going, what projects it supports, and what its foundational political ideology is — and, therefore, how the work of its local affiliates support the national network's goals.

National Alinskyian networks don't advertise the organizational hierarchy but it isn't a secret. In 1996, an *Evaluation Study of Institution-Based Organizing* prepared for the Discount Foundation states:

---

[96] "Jack Egan Interview," *Social Policy*, November/December 1980.

[97] Ernesto Cortes, "Organizing the Community: The Industrial Areas Foundation Organizer Speaks to Farmers and Farm Activists," *The Texas Observer*, July 11, 1986.

[W]hile IAF does not present itself as a national network, its affiliates are clustered into regions, only some of which are acting at state-wide and regional levels. However, IAF did act nationally a few years ago when leaders and organizers from numerous regions met with key congressional leaders in Washington, DC. They influenced Congressional leaders to pressure the INS to speed up applications for citizenship, particularly in California.[98]

One could also point to national economic, housing, and job training projects as well as education and healthcare "reform" to demonstrate massive efforts that go far beyond *local* issues…unless one torturously argues that, as actions on the national level affect every citizen, every national action *is* "local."[99]

Of course, then one must be prepared to explain suppression of local opinion by the national organization. There's a story from San Antonio about the local IAF preparing a "vision paper" on education.[100] They had a national model to follow, although the "150 community leaders" thought they were being original. Originality was the last thing the IAF organizers could allow:

The only discordant note was quickly smothered by Cortes. A priest rose to speak in behalf of the "school

---

[98] Jeannie Appleman, *Evaluation Study of Institution-Based Organizing* prepared for the Discount Foundation, November 12, 1996, p. 16. Http://uac.rdp.utoledo.edu/comm-org/papers97/appleman.htm

[99] These organizational projects will be discussed in detail, in Section 3 – chapters 10-14.

[100] This will be discussed in more detail in a subsequent volume of *Change Agents*.

voucher issue" a means of providing public financing for struggling parochial schools – and one mother seconded his plea.[101] ....Outside in the lobby later, Cortes bluntly warned the priest to back off, lest he provoke an argument that might break up the multi-denominational coalition. "I told the monsignor it was not in his interest to push the voucher issue," Cortes said, "because we would have to fight him on it."[102]

Many other local concerns and issues are not in the "self interest" of the locals to push – because it would mean opposing the national network's agenda.

Once the Alinskyian network has been established as a local affiliate, it offers local leaders advanced training, using values-clarification and "conscientization" (also called popular education) techniques. There are training programs tailored for interested individuals within member institutions and for each member institution's hand-picked leaders.

[T]hey[103] drew explicitly on the religious language and stories of the people. The clarification of individual values with emphasis on living out professed values was begun early in recruitment sessions.[104]

The organizers consciously use "values-clarification" techniques to mold the thinking of their leaders.

Cortes and Drake[105] conducted workshops for the first group of leaders aimed at bringing the values and

---

[101] They publicly were rebuffed by Cortes.
[102] Greider, *Who Will Tell* ...p. 231.
[103] IAF organizers for Valley Interfaith in Texas.
[104] Eklund, *Rhetoric* ...p 82.
[105] IAF organizers working in the Texas Valley Interfaith.

anger of the people to the surface.[106]

The IAF offers extensive (and expensive) 10-day trainings at centers around the country to its more promising leaders.[107]

It was from this group of 'natural' leaders that people were chosen to attend Industrial Areas Foundation workshops. Once these leaders returned to the Valley, they, along with Cortes and Drake, conducted sessions in communities throughout the Valley. The sessions began with a talk about the Valley's historical background, which was followed by value clarification exercises.[108]

Ed Chambers, national director of the IAF, and Cortes believe that values-clarification and controlled, channeled surfacing of anger "provide the momentum for action."[109]

Emphasis is placed on understanding individual values through value clarification exercises, how to use power, the difference between self-interest and selfishness, relationships, especially the differences between public and private relationships, how to organize meetings, and how to use the media. These training sessions are intensive, weeklong workshops where IAF professional organizers utilize many forms of human relations development techniques.[110]

---

[106] Eklund, *Rhetoric* …p 83.
[107] Chapter 15 presents a detailed look at one of these centers.
[108] Eklund, *Rhetoric* …p 83.
[109] Eklund, *Rhetoric* …p 13.
[110] Eklund, *Rhetoric* …p 14.

Values-clarification doesn't help an individual to recognize his personal, philosophical backbone, but is intended to develop a new moral sensibility in him. Specifically, in the case of community organizing, the process is designed to transform generalized "Judeo-Christian" or "American" concepts of cooperation, participation, integrity, free expression, concern, reciprocity, justice, etc., into political activism.[111]

Cold Anger, recommended by the IAF as a fair and accurate report of its work, describes an IAF values-clarification session. In this case, a role-play brings one participant – a pastor – to the point of tears, revealing that he has a son whose life was shattered by meningitis. The organizer draws out the feelings of frustration and impotence, pressing these emotions until the pastor articulates his anger with God and with the "system." "I had insurance," he says, "but now when I go with other families to the hospital with their children, and they don't have any money, I really get angry with the doctors and the politicians."[112]

What has one to do with the other? It doesn't matter – the admission is useful and the author asks, "Why does the minister's doubt express something more spiritual to me than certainty? Why does it have such power?"

It has "power" because the illogical blaming of "the doctors" is used to move this minister into political activism, as defined by the organizer. The corrosion of his faith has been encouraged; God has failed and Man must fight to set things right and "change the system" through community organizing.

"The values-clarification process destroys faith and hope," its critics claim.[113] The participant is guided to experience

---

[111] Eklund, *Rhetoric* ... pp 84-87, 89 give a detailed description of the process.
[112] Mary Beth Rogers, *Cold Anger,* University of North Texas press, 1990. Pp 51-54.
[113] "Understanding the Values Clarification Process," WATCH (PO Box 227, Taneytown, MD 21787), June 1994, p. 11.

overwhelming feelings but is then hindered from comforting himself with uncritical expressions of his values.

Unless, at that emotionally-charged moment, he has the intellectual fortitude to articulate his beliefs, he is vulnerable to suggestion. The idea that organizing one's community will relieve personal powerlessness in the face of pain sounds reasonable. Action can be analgesic and the victim of conscientization never realizes what has been stolen.[114]

Alinskyian community organizations hold massive rallies (conventions) to demonstrate their "power" and establish organizational identity among their members.

Larry McNeil, the West Coast regional director of the IAF,

---

[114] For the reader who is interested in further information about various manipulative psychological techniques or processes, the following short bibliography may be useful:

- Dr. Bill Coulson, "Repentant Psychologist: How I Wrecked the IHM Nuns," *The Latin Mass, Chronicle of Catholic Reform,* 1994). This article is Coulson's heartbreaking public confession of his work among religious sisters, using techniques developed by Carl Rogers.
- Judith Ammenhauser, "The Values Clarification Process," *Mother's Watch,* June 1994.
- Ann Wilson, *Pavlov's Children: A Study of Performance-Outcome-Based Education,* 1994.
- Bev Eakman, *Educating For the New World Order - The Role of Behavioral Psychology, Halcyon House,* 1991.

Of Names to explore:

- Kurt Lewin, a German psychologist known for developing a three-fold process of reeducation ("change process").
- Sydney Simon," one of the fathers of values clarification and author of *Values Clarification: A Handbook for Teachers and Students.*
- Dr. Louis E. Raths, another pioneer in values clarification, "child empowerment," and the author of *Values and teaching: working with values in the classroom*
- Popular education

calls them "ritual" actions, which he believes are the sustenance of his organization. After describing a Roman Catholic Mass, "in which every person present participates in the mystery of the faith," McNeil explains how ritual is consciously incorporated into the IAF:

> The defining IAF ritual has been the Briefing-Action-Evaluation. It is the IAF liturgy, our central practice in the training and development of leaders and organizers. The tight, focused meeting is a second ritual. Anywhere you go in the country you know you are in an IAF meeting because it is short, clear, participatory, and aimed toward action. Our national ritual is 10-day training, probably the key element in our expansion and success since the mid-1970s.[115]

A description of these rituals as performed by the Texas Valley Interfaith says:

> 'Actions' are staged events and are always carefully rehearsed and ritualistic...these actions were conducted like a political caucus or convention, with banners, balloons, billboards and signs."[116]

Alinskyian community organizations use some rallies – which they call "accountability sessions" – to push politicians to support their projects.

> The elaborately charged "accountability" sessions of the IAF groups have become notorious. Officeholders are usually seated on a stage in an auditorium facing

---

[115] Larry B. McNeil, "The Soft Arts of Organizing," *Social Policy*, Winter 1995.
[116] Eklund, *Rhetoric...* p 55.

several hundred, or even thousands, of church people waving banners and revved up for action. One of the group's leaders reads a statement or asks a series of specific questions, and the officials have only about three to five minutes to respond. There is no time for equivocation. A simple "yes" or "no" is about all that is allowed. Many elected officials talk privately about how much they hate the "adversarial nature" of the sessions, which generate an almost paranoiac dread among some politicians – even at the national level.[117]

Another account provides a similar description with the added information that no candidate dissented from the organizational platform raising the observation that either this was an enormous amount of wasted collective energy to demonstrate "power" over candidates that were already entirely in agreement with the assembly or that an accountability assembly, by its nature, is designed to eliminate dissent:

---

[117] Rogers, *Cold Anger*...p 27-28; The description of a MICAH (Gamaliel affiliation) accountability session sounds even more aggressive. John Goldstein observed, "The MICAH ministers really got tough. They pulled microphones away from elected officials, and they did a traditional community organizing thing, where they said, 'Will you support the CBA, yes or no?' And when politicians started giving speeches, an older minister took the mic [sic] away. County supervisors were screaming, and we had coalition partners who were freaked. One said, 'Look, all the work we've done has gone out the window—the county board's mad at us.' It ended up being the county board that was strongest in the end, but that was a very tense moment. That summation meeting at the end of the public meeting was very tough—people were in tears. They're not used to dealing with elected officials like that." David S. Dobbie, "More than the Sum of their Parts? Labor-Community Coalitions in the Rust Belt," A dissertation submitted in partial fulfillment of the requirements for the degree of Doctor of Philosophy (Social Work and Sociology) in the University of Michigan, 2008.

At the accountability assembly, London Citizens demanded that the candidates respond to their priorities. "If the mayoral candidates want our votes on 1 May, they have to prove their worth by signing up to our agenda and implementing it when in office," said Sarfraz Jeraj, one of the assembly co-chairs and a community leader from south London....With some minor caveats, the candidates agreed to all of London Citizens' proposals.[118]

Was there really no difference between these four candidates? Not even on controversial topics? The same article continues:

Perhaps most surprising has been the success of Strangers Into Citizens, an audacious campaign [of the United Kingdom IAF] to establish a route into citizenship for irregular migrant workers. When it began two years ago, even some in London Citizens had doubts that it could garner much support. Yet on 9 April all four mayoral candidates endorsed it.

Alinskyian community organizations also engage in "actions", that is, in activities designed to force change. They are predetermined to be "winnable," valuable to larger organizational goals, and carefully researched, orchestrated, and evaluated.

Research entails a thorough assessment of the power structures involved that will help or hinder the goal. Framing

---

[118] Deborah Littman (a trustee of London Citizens, a UK IAF affiliate), "Another politics is possible," *Red Pepper*, 7-5-08; describing a London Citizens' mayoral accountability assembly in April 2008.

the right questions at the "research" stage controls the direction of the action. The research committee of an Alinskyian local will find out any information necessary to discuss its projects in public or with legislators.

After "research," there is a planned "action." In the earlier days of organizing, the action was confrontational. For example, to inspire a recalcitrant bank president to meet with his community organization, activists spent an amusing day at the bank, changing pennies to dollar bills, and dollar bills back into pennies.[119]

As indicated in IAF training material and in journalistic accounts, a reaction is anticipated and much of the preplanning that takes place seeks to elicit a reaction from those attending the action or accountability session.[120]

As the Alinskyian organizational networks age, however, the action is more complex. The IAF:

…not only teaches people specific political details about legislation, issues and the skills to cooperate and act together effectively, it also adds a dynamic intellectual life involving a practical theory of action, employing and constantly developing concepts like power, mediating institutions, public life, the meaning and management of time, judgment, imagination, and self-interest.[121]

---

[119] Boyte, *Commonwealth* … p 116-117, describing BUILD in 1981.
[120] Eklund, *Rhetoric*…p 55-56.
[121] Boyte, *Commonwealth*… p 82.

Teachers, for example, may be organized to visit every family in their class. Parents may be invited to training sessions on a variety of educational topics that the community organization wants them to support. The training itself is an "action."

> A series of training sessions was organized to draw people into dialogue about the current crisis in education, the societal and economic changes that have been occurring in the United States, and what preparation children would need to be able to function effectively in the world when they graduate. These training sessions helped parents and teachers to think critically and creatively about education; more importantly, they helped to strengthen the relationships between the parents and their children's teachers, enabling them to work more closely together.[122]

Examined closely, this ideologically guided "dialogue" has much in common with the popular education of Alinsky and Paulo Freire.[123] Its "critical thinking" is a buzzword for coming to the "right" conclusions, those endorsed by the "People's Organization." Forcing the analysis to explore "societal and economic changes" molds what people will think about the issue of an "educational crisis."

If the analysis had been spiritual, however, it would entertain very different types of solutions. The work of "conscientizing

---

[122] *Engaging the Public" One Way to Organize,* A concept paper produced by the Industrial Areas Foundation for the National Alliance for Restructuring Education, 1994…p 12 (Ernesto Cortes, author)

[123] This will be discussed in more detail in a subsequent volume of *Change Agents.*

the people" is the Alinskyian's most important "action."

2. The Industrial Areas Foundation

Premier among the Alinskyian organizing networks is the one founded by Saul Alinsky in 1940, the Industrial Areas Foundation (IAF).

The IAF is one of several Alinskyian community organizing networks – each of which has dozens of local affiliates around the United States.[124] Its primary members in any given city are faith institutions and schools that, thanks to the trust society invests in them, are creating community support for "systemic change."

The systemically altered society is already well under way. Federal Empowerment Zone and Enterprise Communities grants for economic development require that cities submit *sustainable development* plans, prepared with the input of community organizations such as the IAF. These federal dollars obligate the participating community to demonstrate a commitment to a comprehensive package of development: education reform, expanded health and social services coverage, school-to-work and similar job training and placement programs, housing, environmental care, etc. The sustainable models on which these plans are drawn are ultimately statist.

As the IAF movement toward systemic change has occurred, to a large degree, within faith institutions, the most serious ramifications of Alinskyian community organizing are theological. The IAF's influence is "liberationist." Prayer and religious symbols are used for the IAF's own organizational ends, and scripture frequently is "spun" to lend support to organizational actions. The IAF promotes a "political" ethics,

---

[124] A current list of IAF affiliates can be found at its website: www.industrialareasfoundation.org.

namely that "the ends justify the means," and teaches morality-by-consensus. These three characteristics of the IAF — repurposing religious elements for secular purposes, Machiavellian public actions, and moral relativism — are features of liberation theology, as well.

FORMING THE INDUSTRIAL AREAS FOUNDATION

The success of the Back of the Yards, Alinsky's organizing effort in Chicago during the 1930s interested a number of progressive-minded philanthropists, one being Marshall Field. In order to bankroll Alinsky's work, Field and several other well-to-do associates created a foundation — the Industrial Areas Foundation, specifically — to enable their donations to be tax-deductable. [125]

This enabled Alinsky to establish a small office in Chicago as a base of operations from which he oversaw community-organizing efforts around the country and built political relationships. The IAF's first board of directors included Field, Bishop Bernard Sheil of Chicago, and the daughter of John Lewis, the powerful head of the labor movement's Congress of Industrial Organizations (CIO).

The presence of Bishop Sheil on the IAF board was only one of many consequential connections between Alinsky and the Catholic Church. In the early 40s, Alinsky met and found a strong ally in Msgr. John O'Grady, Director of the National Conference of Catholic Charities. [126] He became fast friends of the French Catholic philosopher Jacques Maritain during the years Maritain lived in the US to escape the ravages of World

---

[125] Sanford D. Horwitt, *Let Them Call Me Rebel: Saul Alinsky, His Life and Legacy*, Vintage Books (NY, 1989), p 86.
[126] *Let Them...*p 260.

War II. [127]

Through Maritain, Alinsky met the Chicago priest Jack Egan in 1954. Egan became one of Alinsky's most successful – and influential – disciples. [128]

AFTER ALINSKY

Ed Chambers, a Catholic ex-seminarian, became the IAF director after Alinsky's death in 1972. [129] He not only changed certain structural elements in the IAF but effected deeper, more serious alterations.

On the more superficial level, the changes Chambers brought to the IAF rendered it more business-like. Alinsky had envisioned a pool of trained organizers he could send around the country but at the time of his death, only a handful of those with whom he had worked so hard remained in the organization. Chambers understood the organizers' problems and offered them "competitive" salaries so that when their youthful idealism encountered the demands of a family, they would not be driven out of organizing because of pragmatic necessity.

He also realized that one reason Alinsky's organizations had floundered was that, despite the emphasis on grassroots

---

[127] Bernard Doering, editor, *The Philosopher and the Provocateur,* University of Notre dame Press (Notre Dame, 1994), p. xviii.

[128] *The Philosopher and the Provocateur*…pp 61-62, refer to an unpublished letter from Maritain to Alinsky (1-27-54) that appears to encourage Alinsky to call Egan. Margery Frisbie's *An Alley in Chicago: The Ministry of a City Priest* (which is a biography of Jack Egan), gives an account of their meeting in chapters 6-7.

[129] Chambers retired as executive director in January 2010. The four co-directors of the IAF – Ernesto Cortes and Mike Gecan in 2010; Sr. Christine Stephens and Arnie Graf in 2011 – assumed his responsibilities in the years immediately following Chamber's tenure.

leadership, much of their energy and direction was provided by the professional organizer who knew how to keep people stirred up and engaged. Chambers scrapped Alinsky's "three years and you're out" principle and assigned organizers to each IAF local for as long as it was expedient.

Another of Chambers' changes, however, would have angered Alinsky. Joan Lancourt wrote that Alinsky was adamant that his organizations should be locally focused.[130] Fearing what he called fascism, or the centralization of government, Alinsky sought to counter it with a people's movement that would "restore democracy at the local level".[131]

Organizers who insisted on connecting community development to national or international activism needed to find work elsewhere. "When one organizer took a group of members to a Poor People's Convention in Newark, sponsored by the SDS [Students for a Democratic Society], he was promptly fired."[132] The man had felt the housing problems in Syracuse involved "structural and institutional" considerations and was prepared to guide his people according to those assumptions. Alinsky would have none of it.

Chambers, on the other hand, developed the IAF precisely to respond to those "structural and institutional" problems on the national, and international, level. By the early 1990s, the IAF had veered 180° from Alinsky's idea of democratic People's Organizations, although the IAF continued to use that language.

> In order to imagine a restored democracy, one has to imagine a politics beyond cities and states that can

---

[130] Joan Lancourt, *Confront or Concede: The Alinsky Citizen-Action Organizations*, (Lexington: Lexington Books, 1979).

[131] *Confront…* p 32.

[132] *Confront…* p 34.

speak convincingly to the national government in
Washington....

In their cautious, deliberate manner, the IAF
organizations are trying to develop channels with
which to speak in unison on larger national or regional
questions. For the past couple of years, Andres
Sarabia and key leaders from other cities have been
meeting regularly in Washington with their
congressional delegations, exploring the landscape of
national legislative politics, trying out modest
proposals and establishing relationships with those in
power.

These contacts are only a first step and IAF now intends to
expand its national base more rapidly. Cities in virtually every
region of the nation have urged the organization to come in and
help repair local politics. Arnie Graf, recruiting for the
expansion, explained the strategy:

Generally our hope is [quoting IAF mid-Atlantic
regional director] that by 1996, we would be in twice
the strategically located states as we are now [1992]
and that would give us the capacity to develop either
the regional or national base to look at national
policies. If we were in the right fifteen or sixteen
states, we wouldn't have to be in all fifty states. That
would give us enough clout to affect policies, whether
it was through political parties or corporations.[133]

[133.] William Greider, *Who Will Tell the People*, (New York: Simon and Schuester,
1992), pp. 236-237

In 1993, there were around 23 IAF locals. At the beginning of 1996, there are over 40. Twelve years later, there are about 60. Clearly, the IAF's long-term, strategic plans have been on target.

Further, under Alinsky, neighborhoods were organized for the purpose of developing local awareness and building relational bridges. COPS in San Antonio, Texas, along with all the other neighborhood rivals it spawned and Back of the Yard in Chicago with its numerous imitators, originally had a certain legitimacy in that community people were genuinely addressing community concerns from their own perspective. The fact that the organization was sometimes at serious odds with its IAF organizers was a demonstration that the groups could develop self-direction and independence. When the "educationals" of the Community Service Organizations in California sparked internal organizational fireworks, Alinsky saw it as a sign of inner health. That the FIGHT could muddle itself into oblivion after the IAF left it on its own, meant that indeed, it was on its own.

The contemporary IAF, with its "national and regional questions" cannot risk the quirky individualism of an independent, self-governing local. Organizational policy comes from the top and the locals must be "educated" into "consensus." The IAF's function as a "change agent" for developing local acceptance of "educational reform" would be an example of this.[134]

Another significant departure the present IAF has made from Alinsky's organization, and perhaps its most serious, is its increased blending of religion and politics. Alinsky "had wanted his organizers to have ideas and suggestions, but he didn't want them to start pushing people around to make their personal

---

[134] This will be discussed in more detail in volume II of *Change Agents*.

vision come true".[135] That applied to religion, too. Msgr. Jack Egan recalled Alinsky as having said to the organizers who approached their work with evangelical zeal, "Lookit. We'll do the organizing; you take care of the religion." Egan was one of the organizers who wanted more control over people, however, and he continued, "I could never convince him they were one and the same thing…"[136]

Of course, Alinsky "used" the Church unabashedly as a source of money and pre-collected membership but he recognized that a religious institution's utility to him required it to be autonomously healthy and effective within its own sphere.[137]

The current crop of organizers is not as perceptive. Egan quoted Ernesto Cortes, present southwest regional director of the IAF, as saying, "The people we're working with are a deeply religious people. And we should enable them to reflect upon the gospel as it applies."[138]   That is, as the organizer applies it, which is the wolf, not the pastor, preaching to the sheep.

CALL TO ACTION

Therefore, far from respecting the religious institutions it organized, the post-Alinsky IAF actively sought to change them, structurally and ideologically – particularly the Catholic Church. In 1976, Catholic delegates from around the United States met in Detroit at a conference sponsored by the US Conference of Catholic Bishops but openly controlled by Alinskyian organizers.

The theme was "A Call to Action," but Father Vincent Miceli

---

[135] *Radical Vision…*, p 255.
[136] "Interview with Jack Egan," *Social Policy*, November, December 1980.
[137] This will be discussed in more detail in volume II of *Change Agents*.
[138] "Interview with Jack Egan…"

wrote that its true theme was a "Call to Revolution." The conference "recommended changes" in the Catholic Church that ranged from shifting the Church hierarchy to more "democratic" governance, to demands that doctrines regarding contraception, abortion, the right to private property and national defense, and the right of reasonable profit be abandoned. People who eschewed Church teachings about marriage were to be permitted Communion, women were to be ordained as priests and bishops, socialism and pacifism were to be proclaimed doctrinally true and morally good practice, and priests were to be allowed to marry. All of these were specific, actual demands that Call to Action made on the Catholic Church. A bishop at the conference who attempted to protest was told, "You came here to listen, not to talk".[139]

Another observer wrote, "[H]onest opposition [was] cut off crudely and silenced. Opponents of ruling radicals were told to 'stop debating points, to cease referring to encyclicals, council documents and traditional teachings.'"[140] They were warned to "lay aside philosophical definitions and disciplined, coherent thinking;" they wanted input that emphasized experience and social concern.[141] There was no debate, no discussion.

John Cardinal Krol lamented, "Rebels have taken over the conference...[It is] being manipulated by a few people..."[142]

Father Miceli, an eyewitness, called the 3-day conference a

[139.] Fr. Vincent Miceli, "Detroit: A Call to Revolution in the Church", *Homiletic and Pastoral Review*, March 1977, quoting Russell Kirk, *National Review*, December 10, 1976.

[140] "Detroit: A Call to Revolution ...," quoting Kenneth A. Briggs, *New York Times*, October 27, 1976, speaking of pre-conference "hearings."

[141.] "Detroit: A Call to Revolution ...," quoting Kenneth A. Briggs, *New York Times*, October 27, 1976, speaking of pre-conference "hearings.

[142.] "Detroit: A Call to Revolution...,"quoting from the *Detroit Free Press*, Saturday, October 23, 1976.

"carefully orchestrated, militantly controlled media event."[143]

Another commentator said, "One of the phenomena of Detroit was that it was a political meeting...the whole setting from badges and delegate status to observer status, press corps; the whole slick political convention mode was the one that conveyed a message to you: that it was really politics as religion."[144]

Who was behind this?

The organizers of this conference, not surprisingly, included Msgr. Jack Egan of the IAF[145] and Cardinal Deardon, who had been the primary ecclesiastical promoter for establishing the Campaign for Human Development, a Catholic "charitable" collection to fund Alinskyian organizing.[146] Nine volumes of preliminary material, "working papers" on specific aspects of "Call to Action" positions had been prepared before the conference began.[147] Not too surprisingly, within the "working papers" was a specific "call" to support both the Campaign for Human Development and a San Antonio IAF local, Communities Organized for Public Service. In fact, that particular IAF local had been involved the year before in conducting a pre-Detroit consultation on *Nationhood,* one of the

---

[143] "Detroit: A Call to Revolution..."

[144.] James Twyman, *"The Betrayal of the Citadel,"* (Portland: Viva il Papa, Inc., 1978), pg. 23.

[145] Monsignor Jack Egan of Chicago, "a longtime Alinsky supporter, IAF board member, and activist on Chicago urban issues," [*The Neighborhood Works*], served as co-chair of the 1976 Call to Action plenary sessions.

[146] This will be discussed in more detail in volume II of *Change Agents.*

[147] The position papers were on the topics of 1) Nationhood, 2) Neighborhood, 3) Family, 4) Humankind, 5) Personhood, 6) Ethnicity, 7) Church, and 8) Work. They are described in a number of places, one being the *Call to Action* "Working Papers: Introduction," NCCB, undated (circa 1976).

many topics addressed by the "Call to Action" convention. The *Nationhood* working papers envisioned a political system in which faith-based community organizing would:

- establish priorities for public policy
- define major election issues
- educate the Church on the moral dimensions of public issues, and
- implement these goals with other churches and civic groups.

Another working paper, *Neighborhoods,* took up the call for systemic change and insisted that every parish financially support competent neighborhood/community action groups. To accomplish this, the "working papers" contained specific challenges to the discipline and doctrine of the Church.

> [M]ore than 2,400 delegates at the conference — people deeply involved in the life of the institutional church and appointed by their bishops — approve such progressive resolutions, ones calling for, among other things, the ordination of women and married men, female altar servers, and the right and responsibility of married couples to form their own consciences on the issue of artificial birth control. [148]

James Twyman wrote that the role of Alinskyism in that first Call to Action conference was pervasive and unmistakable. "[T]he meeting in Cobo Hall [the 1976 Call to Action conference] brought to life the methods and morality of the Saul

---

[148] Heidi Schlumpf, "Remembering the First Call to Action Conference," *The New World News*, September 20, 1996.

Alinsky handbooks, *Reveille for Radicals* and *Rules for Radicals*."[149] Whatever may have been the mitigating features of Alinsky's thought, they were no longer present to shield the Church from the raw conclusions IAF-trained religious and laity drew and exercised. The cavalier rejection of "truth," the high sounding talk about the will of "the people," the heady conversations about "means" and "tactics" were no longer understood through the lens of Alinsky's idealism; "participatory education," coalition-building, strategies of restructuring – not only for the Church but for the entire nation – were the explicit goals of these very serious radicals.

The years following the first "Call to Action" conference have seen careful, methodical spread of church-based IAF locals. Msgr. Jack Egan, an IAF board member until his death in 2007, continued as a spokesman for the Call to Action agenda until his death in 2001.[150] The 1996 Call to Action calendar showed that IAF Southwest Regional Director, Ernesto Cortes, was a guest speaker at CTA workshops, [151] and Our Lady Queen of Angels Catholic Community in Texas, a member of IAF local Valley Interfaith, has been listed as a Call to Action participating community.[152]

---

[149] *"The Betrayal of the Citadel,"* p. 57.

[150] Heidi Schlumpf, "Remembering the First Call to Action Conference," *The New World News*, September 20, 1996.

[151] Call to Action web page http://listserv.american.edu/catholic/cta.

[152] Other examples are: The Southwest Austin Christian Community of St. Ignatius Martyr Church is listed as a Call to Action participating community [see Exhibit 13]. The Southwest Austin Christian Community, through St. Ignatius Martyr Church, is a member of Austin Interfaith. [Buena Vista News, 1998, p. 5. http://www.buenavista.org/Buena1.html.; Member congregations of Austin Interfaith www.auschron.com/issues/vol14/issue46/pols.interfaith.members]; The Center for Action and Contemplation in Albuquerque, New Mexico is listed

Catholics resisted being organized with varying degrees of intensity and so the organizers modified their approaches, softened their confrontational tactics, and polished their professionalism. Shunning publicity, looking respectably middle-class, as taught by Alinsky, they made a great effort to blend in and to become acceptable, mainstream entities, no more unusual than the local certified public accountant or neighborhood consultant.

But the IAF continues to insinuate itself in the internal life of the Catholic Church. [153] For example, Peter Skerry reports that the IAF was involved in the election of a Texas bishop: "Fundamental to the success of COPS [San Antonio IAF local] has been the support of Archbishop Flores, himself the beneficiary of a COPS letter writing campaign when the

---

as a Call to Action participating community. It is a member of the IAF local, Albuquerque Interfaith. [Call to Action Renewal Directory, 1998 Internet Edition, New Mexico listings; Albuquerque Interfaith information for the year 1994: List of dues-paying members]; St. Odilia Catholic Church in Tucson, Arizona is an institutional member of IAF local affiliate PIMA County Interfaith. In March 1998, St. Odilia hosted a Future of Priestly Ministry Dialogue, a joint project of Call to Action and FutureChurch. [1995 Listing of PIMA County Interfaith Council member organizations demesan.simplenet.com/pcic1/members.html; *Call to Action Newsbriefs, ChurchWatch*, May 1998. call-to-action.org/watch5-98/briefs]; Holy Family in Inverness, Illinois is a member of the IAF local affiliate, United Power for Action and Justice. The pastor of Holy Family, Reverend Patrick Brennan, is a popular Call to Action speaker. [Holy Family Parish Bulletin, October 5, 1997, letter from the pastor, Pat Brennan; 1996 Call to Action Conference listing of focus sessions, including "Traditions and McChurch" by Patrick Brennan.]

[153] The IAF is not the only Alinskyian organizing network with ties to the dissident Catholic movement Call to Action. When Ruth Kolpack, president of JOB (Justice Overcoming Borders), a Gamaliel affiliate in Wisconsin, got herself into doctrinal trouble, Call to Action issued a public statement in her defense. The founding director of Interfaith Worker Justice, Kim Bobo, is a Call to Action speaker.

---

hierarchy was considering his appointment."[154]

In the Archdiocese of Los Angeles, community organizing is "recognized as an integral aspect of parish ministry."[155] The Archdiocesan Office of Justice and Peace terms community organizing a "social justice ministry" and encourages parishes to financially support sending their parishioners to "intensive training in organizing and advocacy work. The social justice ministry.... is funded at the same level of other parish ministries, such as liturgy and music. The parish gives social justice leaders many skills and training opportunities. The parish may be a member of a community organizing group, such as IAF or PICO, and parishioners receive intensive training in organizing and advocacy work. The parish may also be involved in interfaith advocacy work."[156]

The Archdiocese of Los Angeles isn't unique in this open integration of its spiritual mission with an Alinskyian organizing agenda. The Archdiocese of Chicago, which has poured millions of dollars into the IAF affiliate United Power for Action and Justice (UPAJ), mandates that "parish leaders are [to be]

---

[154] Peter Skerry, "Neighborhood COPS," *New Republic,* February 6, 1984.

[155] Archdiocese of Los Angeles, Synod of Los Angeles, Initiatives (the Synod "engaged a process of identification, refinement, and selection, resulting in the realization of six Pastoral Initiatives, nine Pastoral Priorities (seven of first priority rank and two of second priority rank), and fourteen Pastoral Strategies")
www.archdiocese.la/synod/initiatives/other.html.

[156] www.la-archdiocese.org/ministry/justice/peace/pdf/SocialJusticeParishSchema.pdf; Los Angeles Auxiliary Bishop Edward Clark has claimed that "gospel-based community organizing is one of the four legs of parish ministry; the others are liturgy and prayer, catechesis and education, and charity." (Ellie Hidalgo, "'People of commitment' seek change," *The TIDINGS,* Diocesan paper of the Archdiocese of Los Angeles, 1-30-04)

involved in community organizing or community-based economic development projects supported through the Catholic Campaign for Human Development." [157]

The first section of the Archdiocese of Santa Fe's 2006 *Pastoral Plan,* which demands "comprehensive justice education for children, youth, adults, and families," includes "ecumenical" community organizing within parishes. Under the heading of "Coordination and Funding," the Pastoral Plan names groups with which it will "cooperate," including Albuquerque Interfaith, an IAF affiliate identified by the Albuquerque Journal as a political vehicle for religious liberals. [158] Albuquerque Interfaith's first organizer, an ex-priest, was recorded saying: "…[I]f you give me 50 names of other people in this congregation who you think I should talk to…I'll go talk to them in that period of time, and see what kind of story we're getting: how do we feed that into the RENEW." [159] RENEW is a program used by the Catholic Church to foster "spiritual renewal." What was here proposed was to piggyback community organizing onto the RENEW program as an example of "faith in action."

One could multiply these examples but they suffice to make the point that Alinskyian organizing is more than "mere politics." [160]

---

[157] Archdiocese of Chicago, Office for Evangelization, "The Parish Mandate: Becoming an Evangelizing Parish," www.goingforth.org/plandoc-part3p3.html

[158] "Our Hearts were Burning Within Us: *Pastoral Plan* for the Archdiocese of Santa Fe," www.archdiocesesantafe.org/ASFPastoralPlan2006.pdf; "Left Flexes Its Muscles," *Albuquerque Journal,* 7- 9-06.

[159] Tim McCluskey, Albuquerque Interfaith Leadership Development Workshop, Our Lady of Guadalupe Church, June 15, 1996.

[160] In subsequent chapters, we will examine the presence of various Alinskyian organizing networks among other religious bodies.

4. ACORN: The Association of Community Organizations for Reform Now

ALINSKYIAN ROOTS

Before Saul Alinsky's death, while the Industrial Areas Foundation was still under his directorship, there were several experiments with different structural models for IAF community organizations.

Each has advantages. Organizing by institutions – particularly religious bodies – provides for immediate respectability. It does, however, force the community organization to be more cautious about expressing itself, for fear of losing membership to controversy. By contrast, organizing one person at a time may be laborious but it does permit the community organization to be more open about its beliefs – the membership has joined in full knowledge and agreement.

ACORN, an acronym for the Association of Community Organizations for Reform Now, considers itself the nation's largest community organization.[161] Unlike most of the major Alinskyian networks, however, which organize through institutions,[162] ACORN prefers individual membership. Gary

---

[161] www.acorn.org/index.php?id=2703: "ACORN, the Association of Community Organizations for Reform Now, is the nation's largest community organization of low- and moderate-income families, working together for social justice and stronger communities. Since 1970, ACORN has grown to more than 350,000 member families, organized in 850 neighborhood chapters in over 100 cities across the U.S. and in cities in Argentina, Peru, Mexico, the Dominican Republic and Canada."

[162] Called "faith-based" or "broad-based" organizing, depending on whether the majority of its institutional members are religious bodies or not.

Delgado, one of ACORN'S four founders,[163] who wrote about his experiences with the organization in his doctoral dissertation from the University of California at Berkeley, implies ACORN went this route for humanizing reasons. "When asked to define the differences between ACORN and the Industrial Areas Foundation (IAF), an ACORN leader in Houston replied, 'ACORN organizes communities; we don't organize industrial areas.'"[164]

Whatever their structural differences, all Alinskyian networks are grounded in the thought of Saul Alinsky and were founded under his influence. ACORN's story begins with the work of George Wiley, another of its four founders. Wiley taught at Syracuse University in New York in 1960 and founded the Syracuse chapter of CORE (Congress for Racial Equality). [165] He quit teaching for full-time organizing and, under the influence of Frances Fox Piven and Richard Cloward, professors from Columbia University School of Social Work, founded the National Welfare Rights Organization (NWRO) in 1966. Delgado, who worked under Wiley as a NWRO organizer[166], describes Cloward and Priven's influence on Wiley:

> Cloward and Priven argued that the poor could
> be mobilized onto the welfare rolls, precipitating
> a political and fiscal crisis. The author gave three

---

[163] The four ACORN founders were George Wiley, Wade Rathke, his brother Dale Rathke, and Gary Delgado.

[164] Gary Delgado, *Organizing the Movement: The Roots & Growth of Acorn,* Temple University Press, 1986, p. 13; information taken from Delgado's biography posted at the Applied Research Center website, of which he is the founder and executive director (www.arc.org).

[165] In 1964, Wiley left Syracuse University and became CORE's associate national director. He then left CORE to found the Poverty/Rights Action Center (P/RAC) in Washington, D.C.

[166] Delgado's biography, posted at the Applied Research Center website (www.arc.org).

reasons why their strategy would succeed. First, their mobilization would guarantee immediate economic benefits. Second, the strategy did not ask people to go outside their immediate experience or be involved in formal organizational roles. Third, the prospects for mass influence were enhanced by the plan's practical basis for coalition between poor whites and poor blacks.

George Wiley, chairman of Syracuse CORE, was impressed by Cloward and Priven's argument. In a 1966 speech, Wiley stated, "This idea of releasing the potential for major economic pressure through trying to encourage people to gain their rights in the welfare system is one that has had immediate response and has been enormously attractive to activists working in urban areas."[167]

The NRWO trained its organizers in an Alinskyian program at Syracuse University's Community Action Training Center.[168] The Community Action Training Center began in 1965, thanks to a generous grant from the federal government and the efforts

---

[167] *Organizing*...p. 23-24 (referencing Frances Fox Piven and Richard Cloward, "The Weight of the Poor: A Strategy to End Poverty," *The Nation,* May 2, 1966) (referencing Frances Fox Piven and Richard Cloward, *Poor People's Movements: Why They Succeed and How They Fail*, [NY: Pantheon, 1977] p278.)

[168] David Walls, "Power to the People: Twenty Years of Community Organizing," adapted from *The Workbook*, 1994; *Organizing*...p 24.

of Warren Haggstrom, a social-work professor.[169] Saul Alinsky was hired as a consultant for the program, to teach seminars and lead community organization actions four days a month. A second organizer from Alinsky's IAF staff, Fred Ross, gave Haggstrom full-time help to run the program.[170]

However, the NRWO, focused solely on welfare rights, was too limited for the organizers' needs. By the early 1970s, Wiley had started ACORN in Arkansas.[171] He wrote, "a political majority can be organized around a common set of fundamental economic issues such as tax reform, health care, and adequate income."[172]

Wiley dispatched a young organizer, Wade Rathke, whom he had trained while organizing for the NWRO.[173] Rathke, like several other community organizers of his era, had been a member of the radical Students for a Democratic Society

---

[169] *Let Them Call Me Rebel*...p. 478. Haggstrom received $314,000 in federal grants to establish The Syracuse University Community Action Training Center. See also: "Syracuse U Won't [Renew] Anti-Poverty Contract with Activist Saul David Alinsky," *Canadian Jewish Review*, 12-31-65. The NWRO had private of financing, too. Marvin Olasky, ex-communist and author of *The Tragedy of American Compassion* writes that from 1968 to 1971, NWRO received more than $500,000 from the National Council of Churches.

[170] Premilla Nadasen, *Welfare Warriors: The Welfare Rights Movement in the United States,* (NY: Routledge), 2005, p. 84

[171] The exact date of ACORN's inception is debatable. Rathke and Wiley began the *Arkansas Community Organizations for Reform Now* (same acronym, with the first letter standing for "Arkansas" rather than "Associations," as it does today) in 1970 (*Organizing*...p. 3). The organization wasn't incorporated until 1977, however (Matthew Vadum, "ACORN: Who Funds the Weather Underground's Little Brother?" Foundation Watch, Capital Research Center, 11-08, p. 8).

[172] *Organizing*...p 25 (referencing George Wiley, "Building a New Majority: The Movement for Economic Justice," *Social Policy*, September/October 1973).

[173] Wade Rathke Biography: www.waderathke.com.

(SDS).[174]

SOCIALIST IDEOLOGY, THE "PEOPLE'S PLATFORM," AND POLITICS

ACORN has always been open about its progressive political activity, which is perhaps one of the advantages of organizing individuals rather than institutions. Promotional material on its website has stated. "Major campaigns, whether around housing, or jobs, or voter registration, are designed to reach the unorganized majority of low and moderate-income people – the key constituency that must be mobilized for a progressive movement for social change in this country to succeed."[175]

ACORN views political action to be an essential part of this mobilization. "While many community organizations are content to sit on the sideline on election day, ACORN members have always used the electoral arena to press their issues. We run successful initiative campaigns, registered half a million voters [as of 1997] and elected our own members to public office."[176] Running and supporting political candidates has been a consistent element of ACORN's work, for instance its endorsement of Barack Obama in the 2008 presidential campaign[177] and Al Franken in his 2008 run for the US Senate.[178]

---

[174] See Chapter 8 for more history about this connection.

[175] ACORN website home page, www.igc.apc.org/community, accessed 3-3-97.

[176] ACORN," website home page...1997.

[177] "Because of Obama's record of working for positive change that helps working families, ACORN Votes, a federal PAC made up of ACORN leaders, endorsed Obama's candidacy for President." www.acorn.org/?id=17856

[178] "Minnesota ACORN Endorses Al Franken," Posted in Press Releases on July 16th, 2008, blog.alfranken.com/2008/07/16/minnesota-acorn-endorses-al-franken

ACORN's political machine has developed Political Action Committees to interview candidates for public office and to endorse the acceptable ones. Historically ACORN PACs have "made decisions on how to urge their members to vote on referenda issues. They encouraged ACORN members to run for office and move the ACORN agenda from the inside of the political system. Their goal was accountability to ACORN voters who supported political leaders and wanted good representation of their interests and goals."[179]

ACORN also uses electoral campaigns to apply pressure "during the nomination campaign when [candidates] were in most need of grassroots support - a specialty of ACORN."[180] For instance, it scheduled its own convention "to coincide with the National Democratic Party conference" where it conducted "hearings to develop issues for the upcoming Democratic National Convention. At the end of the platform-drafting conference, ACORN convention delegates marched on the Democratic Party conference with the basics of a nine-point 'People's Platform.' They demanded a meeting with President Carter but were only allowed to demonstrate in the street. ACORN, however, had created a permanent presence in national politics, that reached the highest levels of power."

This People's Platform was written in 1978 and ratified in 1979 at ACORN's national convention in St. Louis. The document was revised and re-approved in 1990 at ACORN's national 20th Anniversary Convention in Chicago and is in effect at present.[181] Among other things, the ACORN *People's Platform* demands that the United States:[182]

---

[179] *"ACORN's 25-Year History,"* page 7.

[180] www.acorn.org

[181] ACORN People's Platform, revised and ratified 1990, www.igc.apc.org/community/people's_platform.html.

[182] The Preamble of the ACORN's People's Platform states: "Enough is enough. We will wait no longer for the crumbs at America's door. We will

-   "create a national health-care system" in which "all medical costs are covered" and in which doctors are provided a medical "education subsidized by the federal government." [section on Health Care, # I & II]
-   "create more housing" by setting a "goal of a million new units of federally subsidized housing per year." [section on Housing, #I]
-   "charge government and big business with the final responsibility for full employment." [section on Work and Workers' Rights, #II]
-   "guarantee a minimum annual family income..." [section on Work and Workers' Rights, #III]
-   develop schools that are "available for community needs, like adult education" and "job training that is linked to specific employment," and which "can provide all support and services that a child cannot receive at home." [section on Education, #II & IV]

To accomplish the goals outlined in its People's Platform, ACORN needed increasing involvement with electoral politics. Its first foray was a modest "Save the City Rally" in 1972 that all candidates for Little Rock Board of Directors were invited to attend. ACORN's Political Action Committee next backed two candidates for Little Rock School Board and then, buoyed by success, ran several ACORN members for office in Illinois,[183] netting them seats on the Pulaski County Quorum Court. Finally, ACORN entered national politics during the 1980

---

not be meek, but mighty…. We demand the changes outlined in our platform and plan."
[183] 1974

Presidential campaign, when it pressured Democrat candidates looking for grassroots support into backing its agenda.[184]

In 1988, ACORN backed Jesse Jackson's Rainbow Coalition, with thirty Jackson delegates on the floor of the Democratic National Convention.[185] During the 1990s, it began Congressional lobbying, boasting that ACORN leadership operates, "…from inside positions of power. ACORN's work on the savings and loan bailout provided effective means of developing and applying power… ACORN members won appointment to the Resolution Trust Corporation to help determine the management of the billions of dollars of assets the government seized."[186]

The 1990s also saw the development of a political alliance of ACORN with the Democratic Socialists of America (DSA), forming a political party called the New Party. National ACORN president, Maud Hurd, along with Dr. Cornel West, an honorary DSA chair as well as a representative from the Reproductive Rights Coalition Fund, were listed as New Party supporters.[187] Bronx ACORN operated a New Party chapter out of its headquarters.[188] In a drive to identify political allies, the New Party held "extensive discussions" in 1994 with "high ranking officials in labor (teamsters, electrical workers, oil workers, bus drivers, etc.); grassroots environmentalists with Greenpeace, Citizens Clearinghouse on Hazardous Waste and Friends of the Earth; community organizations like ACORN and the Industrial Areas Foundation; DSA and Sane/Freeze, and

---

[184] *"ACORN's 25-Year History,"*
www.igc.apc.org/community/ACORN_25_history.html
[185] *"ACORN's 25-Year History,"* page 9.
[186] *"ACORN's 25-Year History,"* page 10.
[187] "A List of New Party Supporters," New Party Website:
http://www.newparty.org/supporters.html. Accessed 2-6-1996.
[188] "New Party Chapter Contacts," New Party Website:
http://www.newparty.org/supporters.html.

scores of important local organizations."[189]

In 1996, New Party alliances with ACORN, the IAF, Sustainable America, and others, were promoting "living wage" campaigns around the country.[190] Ten years later, little was left of the New Party other than a bare website promoting fusion voting, a long-term strategy of changing states' election rules by permitting minor parties "their own ballot line with which they can either endorse their own candidates or endorse the candidates of other parties. Through fusion, minor parties don't have to always compete in the winner-take-all two party system and can avoid 'spoiling' - throwing an election to the most conservative candidate by splitting the votes that might go to two more progressive candidates (ours and another party's)."[191] Supporters of this idea have targeted Connecticut, Maine, New Mexico, and Oregon for legislation supporting a fusion voting system in the state.[192]

ACORN's political activities went on to take myriad other forms. It lobbied at both the state and national level. It ran "Get Out the Vote" drives, through which ACORN racked up an extraordinary record of voter fraud.[193] It networked with other progressives, endorsing, for example, the pro-abortion Fight the

---

[189] "On the Move with the New Party," New Party Progress Report #5, April 1994, http://fireant.com/newparty/new/9-94.html. The Industrial Areas Foundation is also CHD-funded, receiving approximately 16% of the annual national CHD budget between 1992-1995 [Commentary on the Catholic Campaign for Human Development, Wanderer Forum Foundation, 1997, Exhibit 1, Figure A].

[190] "Living Wage and Campaign Finance Reform Initiates," New Party Introduction Packet Information, undated.

[191] www.newparty.org, accessed 7/11/2009.

[192] www.openballotvoting.org, accessed 7/11/2009.

[193] www.rottenacorn.com/activityMap.html has an extensive list of convictions and impending suits against ACORN

Right March in 1996.[194] An ACORN factsheet explained that, "[O]rganizing needs to happen more than ever to counter Right-wing assault"[195] and that member groups were able to "have a voice in setting a national agenda for organizing to fight the right."[196] The United Labor Unions (ULU) became an effective labor-organizing arm of ACORN.[197] ACORN even ran its own candidates.[198] In short, it was a sophisticated a political force.

---

[194]"Organizations Endorsing the Fight the Right March." List taken from the webpage of NOW, www.now.org/issues/right/orglist.html. The Fight the Right Vision and Mission Statement reads: "The Fight the Right Network connects individuals and representatives of organizations working to promote social and economic justice, democracy, and sexual and reproductive freedom by stopping/counteracting the political and religious Right's attempts to suppress freedoms, to undermine the separation of church and state, and to impose religious control of government, education, and public life."[emphasis added. "Vision" and "Mission" of the Fight the Right Network, taken from the Fight the Right Network webpage, www.critpath.org/ftrn/VisionMission.html]

[195] ACORN factsheet, "Who are we? What have we done? Why join? How to join? Employment Opportunities; More Information," undated, p. 4. www.igc.apc.org/community

[196] ACORN factsheet..., page 6. "ACORN: Association of Community Organizations for Reform Now" ACORN home page, informational material, www.igc.apc.org/community

[197] *"ACORN's 25-Year History,"* page 8.

[198] The 1999 election of Illinois ACORN president and Chicago New Party chair, Ted Thomas, to Chicago alderman representing the 15th ward would be a case in point. [Wayne State University Labor Studies Center, "Living Wage Campaigns: An Activists Guide to Organizing a Movement for Economic Justice," www.laborstudies.wayne.edu/Resources/guide2002.pdf] ACORN state chair in Arkansas, Jonnie Pugh, was recruited by the New Party in 1998 to run for city council in Little Rock. [Zach Polett, "Fair Housing Drives New Party Growth in Little Rock," National Housing Institute *Shelterforce Online*, September/October 1998.] In New York, the Working Families Party, which is affiliated with the New Party, was co-chaired by NY ACORN president Bertha Lewis. [Sol Stern, "ACORN's Nutty Regime for Cities,"

EDUCATION REFORM

Similar to IAF endeavors, ACORN was on the forefront of providing parental support to the education reform movement. In 1988, ACORN established the ACORN Schools Office in New York City. Eleven years later, it boasted:

> The Schools Office channels ACORN's nationally recognized expertise in community organizing and provides technical information, education related leadership development, and other resources to the school reform struggles of very low income and working poor families in New York City.[199]

During a workshop in 1995, New York ACORN organizer Jennifer Anderson identified the particular brand of education reform supported by ACORN's educational activism as that promulgated by educator Debbie Meier.[200] NY-ACORN helped establish a number of Meier's alternative "New Visions Schools" within the New York public school system.[201]

The experimental schools designed by NY-ACORN, following

City Journal, Spring 2003, www.cityjournal.org; also "New Party Gains," *The Progressive Populist*, May 1999]

[199] New York ACORN Schools Office, "Secret Apartheid II: Race, Regents, and Resources," May 5, 1997, www.acorn.org/index.php?id=537

[200] Jennifer Anderson, workshop: "School Reform Sweeping the Nation,"25th Campaign for Human Development Anniversary Conference in Chicago, 1995 [audio tape].

[201] As of 1997, these included PS 245, ACORN Community High School, and the Bread and Roses Integrated Arts High School.

the Debbie Meier model, had many attractive features — small teacher-pupil ratios and small student bodies, for example. However, each ACORN "New Visions School" also supported one full-time, paid ACORN organizer, whose duties included organizing parents, class by class.[202] Anderson also revealed ACORN's determination to see that only "progressively-minded" teachers and principals were hired in the New Visions Schools.

Academically, the structure of Debbie Meier's "reform" is quite a departure from classical education. It eliminates standardized testing, for example:

> [T]o put the sort of intense emphasis on standardized testing...meant, in practice, the gearing of curricula specifically to prepare students to pass narrowly focused tests—with little attention to the broader array of skills and critical capacities essential in a real world environment... In contrast... an alternative began to emerge.[203]

Parents and educators had to be re-educated to accept this reform, however (explaining the value of the paid ACORN organizer in each school):

> [F]or democratic school approaches to work necessitated not only changes in the formal structure of education but also effective, skillful training and some clear public commitment to an alternative understanding of educational purposes

---

[202] Stephanie Block, "CHD School Reform: Keeping the 'Fringe' Under Control," *The Wanderer*, September 14, 1995.

[203] Harry C. Boyte, *Commonwealth: A Return to Citizen Politics,* (NY: The Free Press) 1989, p. 106. Chapter 7, about the Baltimore IAF's efforts in school "reform," describes the Debbie Meier/Theodore Sizer model of education.

themselves. [204]

These "educational purposes" were, in part, to "change" the larger system, without defining what is meant by "change:"

> New York ACORN is building toward comprehensive, systemic change on two levels. First, the local efforts around school conditions, performance, and governance eventually grow the constituency for broader reform because the causes of most local problems are embedded in the broader system. [205]

Ten years later, the New York City Coalition for Education Justice, which included NY ACORN, recommended that:

> … all low-performing schools should be transformed into community schools where comprehensive medical, social, and emotional support services are provided to students and their families inside the school, through health clinics, adult education classes, legal services, and more. Community-based and city agencies should be thoroughly integrated into school operations, early warning systems should be established to identify and address student difficulties immediately as they arise, and a strong safety net should be developed to address student and family needs that inhibit or interfere with

---

[204] *Commonwealth*…p. 107.
[205] "Secret Apartheid II…"

learning. Aggressive, comprehensive strategies
such as these are critical to tackle the persistent
inequities in the New York City school system....
[206]

To that end, another "educational purpose" was the training
of a new generation of community organizers. In ACORN's
New Visions School in New York, Local 1199 School for Social
Change:

> [S]tudents analyze public health issues, the
> organization of community groups, the
> development of public policy and the
> international labor movement. Students are
> involved in hands-on activities in order to relate
> classroom learning to community service. These
> activities range from participation in labor and
> community organization movements to service as
> interns at local health care facilities. [207]

The assessment that such programs achieve "the gradual
transformation of our once academically successful education
system into one devoted to training children to become
compliant human resources to be used by government and

---

[206] *Coalition for Education Justice,* "Looming Crisis or Historic Opportunity?
Meeting the Challenge of the Regents Graduation Standards," February 2009.
[207] Fact sheet for Local 1199 School for Social Change, Bronx, NY. This is a
New Visions school. Current "Mission Statement" from the school's website
states: "The Coalition School for Social Change's community of staff and
students dedicates itself to examining social problems, developing social
conscience and working toward social change." www.coalitionschool.org –
accessed 5-13-09.

industry for their own purposes," seems chillingly accurate.[208]

HOUSING

During the Reagan administration years, ACORN launched a campaign to obtain affordable housing.[209] In the light of events twenty years later, it's interesting to read ACORN's description of its initial efforts in this area, which began as an:

> ... illegal (though logical and moral) seizing of the properties - squatting.... ACORN placed [ads] in papers asking 'Do you need a home?' The squatting campaign required a personal commitment to move into a vacant, usually poorly kept house, and refit it for comfortable living. It also involved the risk of arrest if local authorities refused them the legal occupation of the home. Nevertheless, the response was great.... Squatting did not occur under cover of darkness. It was well publicized. This was a part of the political dimension of squatting. First, local officials had to agree not to evict or prosecute squatters. Second, ACORN attempted to legalize the act. Then, local officials were asked to

---

[208] Samuel L. Blumenfeld, Foreword to Charlotte Thompson Iserbyt, *the deliberate dumbing down of America: A Chronological Paper Trail* [sic], Conscience Press, 1999. *"ACORN's 25-Year History..."*also mentions that ACORN created the Rockaways New School and PS 245 in New York and the Nicholson and Mason 21 schools in Chicago. "These small schools were set up as partnerships between parents and teachers to serve the local communities and improve children's education."
[209] 1980-1985

subsidize the costs of squatting in an effort to improve the quality of life of the squatters and their neighbors [as part of a campaign to reclaim the neighborhood from drug dealers and other criminals, ed.]. Through these campaigns, ACORN gained national exposure on housing issues and cemented its reputation as the leading authority on low-income community development."[210]

As the organization became more knowledgeable about working "the system," its tactics changed. It established the ACORN Housing Corporation and pressured banks and state and local governments into supporting "affordable housing" – or, in other words, *subsidized* housing.

To this end, ACORN was a major force behind the Community Reinvestment Act (CRA) created in the late 1970s to force banks to make loans to low-income borrowers. These borrowers were often unable to meet their obligations but, so long as their numbers remained small, banks and the federal government could absorb any losses accrued. Therefore, ACORN claimed the programs were a tremendous success and pushed to expand them, reporting banks for disciplinary measures when they failed to award a sufficient number of subprime mortgages. Three decades later, the system collapsed, motivating a "housing bailout" package to rescue Freddie Mac and Fannie Mae by providing them with an unlimited credit line and feeding millions of dollars back to ACORN.[211]

The Freddie Mac/Fannie Mae programs concern more than

---

[210] *"ACORN's 25-Year History…"* page 6-7.
[211] *"ACORN's 25-Year History…"* details a number of the campaigns ACORN waged to direct government money into housing programs for lower income people.

housing. They funnel money earmarked for housing projects into various progressive causes. For instance, both foundations have given money to the Washington, D.C. chapter of Parents and Friends of Lesbians and Gays (PFLAG-DC) for years.[212] Freddie Mac has awarded grants to the Human Rights Campaign (HRC), the nation's largest gay lobby group, to help homosexual couples adopt children.[213] Fannie Mae has sponsored a number of Gay and Lesbian Alliance against Defamation (GLAAD) events – whose purpose is positive media portrayal of homosexuality.[214] Fannie Mae and Freddie Mac have also made substantial campaign donations to Representative Barney Frank (D-MA),[215] an openly gay congressman who chairs the committee having oversight of Fannie Mae and Freddie Mac.[216]

As mentioned above, besides fighting for passage of the Community Reinvestment Act, ACORN monitored banks' compliance with it.[217] Some analysts contend the CRA policies are in good part to blame for the ensuing housing crisis. Representative Michele Bachmann (R-Minnesota), a member of

---

[212] "Bankrupt Mortgage Giants Freddie Mac, Fannie Mae Give Thousands to Homosexual Groups," PRNewswire-USNewswire, 12-18-08.

[213] "Freddie Mac and Fannie Mae Gave Large Donations to Homosexual Activists Just Before Collapse," LifeSiteNews.com, 12-19-09.

[214] "Bankrupt Mortgage Giants…"

[215] Lindsay Renick Mayer, "Fannie Mae and Freddie Mac Invest in Democrats," 7-16-08, www.opensecrets.org/news/2008/07/top-senate-recipients-of-fanni.html

[216] There is a theory that the fact Herb Moses, a former partner of Frank's, was an executive at Fannie Mae during time Frank was serving on the Committee, might have something to do with it: Michael Barone, "Democrats Were Wrong on Fannie Mae and Freddie Mac," *US News and World Report*, 10-6-08

[217] Susan Lahey, "CRA: More Than A Numbers Game," *Bank Director Magazine*, - 4th Quarter 2005

the House Financial Services Committee, argued that the "housing bailout" package signed into law to rescue Freddie Mac and Fannie Mae with an unlimited credit line not only increased the federal debt but also gave millions of dollars to La Raza and to ACORN.[218]

> Operating in at least 38 states (as well as Canada and Mexico), ACORN pushes a highly partisan agenda, and its organizers are best understood as shock troops for the AFL-CIO and even the Democratic Party. As part of the Fannie Mae reform bill, House Democrats pushed an 'affordable housing trust fund' designed to use Fannie Mae and Freddie Mac profits to subsidize ACORN, among other groups. A version of this trust fund actually passed the Republican House and will surely be on the agenda again next year."[219]

Then there was the federal government's Self-help Homeownership Opportunity Program (SHOP) to fund non-profit organizations (like ACORN) so that they could help those "who otherwise would not become homeowners." One stipulation, however, was that prospective homebuyers "must apply through current SHOP grantees" — of which ACORN, of course, was one.[220]

There was also $1 billion of the 2009 Stimulus Plan in

---

[218] Elizabeth Williamson & Brody Mullins, "Democratic Ally Mobilizes In Housing Crunch: Acorn Leads Drive to Register Voters Likely to Back Obama; New Federal Funds," *Wall Street Journal*, 7-31-08.

[219] "The Acorn Indictments," WSJ 11-3-06

[220] SHOP guidelines for applications and SHOP grantees (as of February 5, 2009) through whom government monies are to be disbursed: www.hud.gov/offices/cpd/affordablehousing/programs/shop/#grantees

Community Development Block Grants and another $4.2 billion in the Neighborhood Stabilization Program.[221] ACORN was involved in these programs, too.[222] Not surprisingly, ACORN campaigned enthusiastically for passage of the Economic Recovery Package.[223]

TRAINING ORGANIZERS

ACORN developed its leadership through ACORN Associates, Inc. and through the Institute for Social Justice. Concerning the former, Gary Delgado writes:

> ACORN Associates, Inc., offered (for a fee) consultation, training, and technical assistance to other [community organization] groups. Its purpose was to utilize the talent of ex-ACORN staff, scattered all over the country, to conduct training and to kick back the money to ACORN.[224]

The Institute offered training, as well.

> [T]he Arkansas Institute for Social Justice (AISJ)—after 1978, simply Institute for Social Justice—was formed to offer week-long training programs in cities across the country to make

---

[221] "House Leadership Unveils $825 Billion Stimulus Plan," *Public Policy Weekly Bulletin*, 1-16-09.

[222] Matthew Vadum, "ACORN's Stimulus," *American Spectator*, 1-27-09.

[223] "ACORN and Allies Launch Nationwide Economic Recovery Campaign," www.acorn.org.

[224] *Organizing*…p 101

money for ACORN and to set up an intern program through which trainees would receive stipends from the Institute while learning community organizing in Little Rock.... The Institute's program...was intended, first, to provide ACORN with a nonprofit, tax-exempt arm, important for securing foundation grants. Second, it would serve as a means of organizer recruitment through both the training sessions and the intern program. Third, it represented ACORN's attempt to hegemonize the field of community organizing by offering training in "principles and techniques of community organizing, drawing particularly from the ACORN model of neighborhood-based organizing."[225]

ERA OF SCANDAL AND POWER

In the 1980s, a bright, young Alinskyian community organizer named Barack Obama was honing his skills as lead organizer of the Developing Communities Project, funded by Chicago's south-side Catholic churches[226] and operating under the Gamaliel Foundation, another Alinskyian network.[227] Obama spent another four years building an organization in Roseland and the nearby Altgeld Gardens public housing complex [228] and then, just before going off to law school in the early 1990s, directed Project Vote, a partner organization of

---

[225] *Organizing*...p 101-2.
[226] Ryan Lizza, "The Agitator," *The New Republic Online*, March 3, 2007 www.pickensdemocrats.org/info/TheAgitator_070319.htm
[227] Chapter 6: Gamaliel
[228] Hank de Zutter, "What Makes Obama Run?" *Chicago Reader*, 12-7-95

ACORN.[229]

Obama was trained by some of the top Alinskyian organizers. One mentor was the ex-Jesuit, Greg Galuzzo, lead organizer for Gamaliel. The Developing Communities Project was an offshoot of Jerry Kellman's Calumet Community Religious Conference. Kellman was also trained by Alinsky.

Meeting with ACORN leaders in November 2007, in the early days of campaigning for US president, Obama reminded them of the past association, saying, "I've been fighting alongside ACORN on issues you care about my entire career. Even before I was an elected official, when I ran Project Vote voter registration drive in Illinois, ACORN was smack dab in the middle of it, and we appreciate your work."[230] ACORN's Political Action Committee, ACORN Votes, endorsed Senator Obama's run for the US presidency in 2008.[231]

ACORN's work, however, was not only controversial…it was frequently on the wrong side of the law. In 2007, *The Seattle Times* reported the biggest voter-registration fraud scheme in Washington history. Three ACORN employees pleaded guilty, and four more were charged for filling out and submitting more than 1,800 fictitious voter-registration cards during a 2006 registration drive in King and Pierce counties."[232]

---

[229] "What Makes Obama Run?"; Search for Voting Rights Organizer- Florida; www.idealist.org/en/job/277712-141

[230] Sam Graham-Felsen, "ACORN Political Action Committee Endorses Obama," Feb 21, 2008 my.barackobama.com/page/community/post/samgrahamfelsen/gGC7zm

[231] Press Release: "ACORN's Political Action Committee Endorses Obama,"2-21-08, www.acorn.org/index.php?id=8539&tx_ttnews[swords]=obama&tx_ttnews[tt_news]=21759&tx_ttnews[backPid]=8538&cHash=f0d91f054a

[232] Keith Ervin, "Three plead guilty in fake voter scheme," *The Seattle Times,* 10-30-2007.

A year later, an ACORN employee in West Reading, Pennsylvania, was sentenced for to up to 23 months in prison for identity theft and tampering with records. A second ACORN worker pleaded not guilty to the same charges and was freed on $10,000 bail.

Other indictments, such as the four ACORN employees in Kansas City charged with identity theft and filing false registrations during the 2006 election or the Reynoldsburg ACORN employee indicted on two felony counts of illegal voting and false registration, after being registered by ACORN to vote in two separate counties, can be added to the list and investigations into ACORN for voter fraud were all over the map. [233] To take a few:

- Milwaukee ACORN was investigated for 200 to 300 fraudulent voter registration cards;
- Cleveland ACORN was investigated for its submission of 75,000 voter registrations, many of which are fraudulent;
- New Mexico ACORN, which claims to have taken 72,000 new voter registrations in the state since January 2008, was under suspicion for 1,100 possibly fraudulent voter registration cards turned in to the Bernalillo County clerk's office.

ACORN's history is riddled with illicit activity. During the 2006 elections, the *Wall Street Journal* carried a story about four ACORN workers who were indicted by a federal grand jury for submitting false voter registration forms to the Kansas City, Missouri, election board. It mentioned that other ACORN workers had been convicted in Wisconsin and Colorado and investigations, at the time the article was written, were under

---

[233] Employment Policies Institute website, www.rottenacorn.com

way in Ohio, Tennessee and Pennsylvania.[234]

Dale Rathke, the brother of ACORN founder Wade Rathke, embezzled nearly $1 million from the organization between 1999 and 2000. It didn't become public, however, until the summer of 2008, thanks to a whistle-blower. According to Maud Hurd, ACORN's president, the incident was handled "in-house," reported on the books of Citizens Consulting, Inc., an ACORN affiliate entity, as a loan. "We thought it best at the time to protect the organization, as well as to get the funds back into the organization.... It was a judgment call at the time, and looking back, people can agree or disagree with it, but we did what we thought was right," Hurd said.[235]

Which brings up yet another fascinating aspect of ACORN — its numerous affiliate and subsidiary organizations, of which Citizens Consulting, Inc. was one.

> Left-wing groups like ACORN often have overlapping memberships and interlocking directorates. They constantly align and realign themselves in short- and long-term strategic coalitions. Sometimes there are formal mergers and sometimes "strategic partnerships." ACORN's tangled family tree includes a host of subsidiaries and affiliated nonprofits that do not have to honor public disclosure laws.

> Blogger Larry Johnson (of "No Quarter") did a LexisNexis corporate filings search for ACORN's southern headquarters at 1024 Elysian Fields

---

[234] "The Acorn Indictments," *Wall Street Journal*, 11-3-06
[235] Stephanie Strom, "Funds Misappropriated at 2 Nonprofit Groups," *New York Times*, 7-9-08

Avenue, New Orleans, Louisiana 70117. He
found that there are an incredible 294 ACORN-
related entities and nonprofits and businesses
using that address. The Employment Policies
Institute has identified more than 100 business
names associated with ACORN. [236]

Therefore, it was extremely difficult to track money flowing
into and out of ACORN. One review of federal spending data
found that ACORN received at least $53 million in federal
money since 1994[237] but there was little accountability for the
money. And a newspaper account from 1987 claimed ACORN
was "run like a Jim Jones cult, where all the money ended up
under Wade Rathke's control and was 'never seen' by the low-
income individuals the organization claims to represent."[238]

Most disturbingly, but not unexpectedly, the federal
government was reluctant to investigate. House Judiciary
Committee Chairman John Conyers, Michigan Democrat,
"backed off his plan to investigate wrongdoing by the liberal
activist group ACORN, saying 'powers that be' put the kibosh
on the idea."[239]

---

[236] Matthew Vadum, "ACORN: Who Funds the Weather Underground's
Little Brother?" *Foundation Watch,* Capital Research Center, 11-08, p. 8-9.
(See noquarterusa.net/blog/2008/10/14/obamas-campaign-liesabout-
acorn/ or http://tinyurl.com/6zkn5d and "The Many Faces of ACORN"
table on page 5 of this report.)
[237] Kevin Mooney, "ACORN got $53 million in federal funds since 94, now
eligible for up to $8 billion more," The Washington Examiner, 5-5-09. A
downloadable spreadsheet of the $53 million is posted at
spreadsheets.google.com/pub?key=r9Nm9MnufdfjwOCnzsefnJQ.
[238] "Board hears wide-ranging criticism of Acorn program, takes no action."
Arkansas Democrat-Gazette. Sept. 2, 1987; "Acorn member resigns from
corporation board." *Arkansas Democrat-Gazette.* Sept. 3, 1987.
[239] S.A. Miller, "Conyers abandons plan to probe ACORN," *The Washington
Times,* 6-25-09.

What law enforcement was reluctant to do, however, public scrutiny achieved. In November 2010, ACORN filed for bankruptcy, although it has planned to reorganize under a new name,[240] according to Matthew Vadum, senior editor at the Capitol Research Center, calling the bankruptcy a "public relations head fake" and a hoax. "ACORN did not die and will not die at the conclusion of the bankruptcy proceeding."[241]

---

[240] Reports of a name change circulated throughout 2009-2010. [See, for example, Kevin Mooney, "ACORN denies name change but former board members remain convinced of re-branding," *Washington Examiner*, 6-24-09.] On a local level, such rebranding had already begun, with NY ACORN becoming NY Communities for Change [Sally Goldenberg, "ACORN shell of itself as it renames office," *New York Post*, 2-23-10], ACORN Housing now called the Affordable Housing Centers of America, and California ACORN now Alliance of Californians for Community Empowerment [Michael Tarn, "ACORN Getting A Makeover: Group Looking For New Name, New Branding After Video Scandal," *Huffington Post*, 3-15-10].

[241] Brian Fitzpatrick, "Watchdog: ACORN bankruptcy a 'hoax': Analyst says radical group plans to come back under a new name," *World Net Daily*, 11-5-10. Another ACORN critic, Judicial Watch, claims that the Obama administration offered $445 million to a former ACORN official, Joe McGavin, to help "unemployed or substantially underemployed" Americans make their mortgage payments. McGavin, formerly director of counseling for ACORN Housing in Chicago and the operations manager for Affordable Housing Centers of America (AHCOA), an ACORN affiliate, now runs Hardest Hit. JW's implication is that Hardest Hit is a thinly veiled reincarnation of an ACORN affiliate, in order to circumvent 2009 legislation that bans federal funding to ACORN. [Corruption Chronicles blog, "Former ACORN Director Gets $445 Mil From U.S. Treasury," Judicial Watch, 6-7-12]

5. PICO National Network

ALINSKYIAN ROOTS

Nearly as large as the *Industrial Areas Foundation* – the prototype of all community organizing – the PICO network has over 50 local affiliates in the United States and several organizing "efforts" in Central America and Rwanda.[242]

PICO is an acronym, originally standing for the Pacific Institute for Community Organization but renamed in 2004 by the PICO National Network, "to reflect its growth as a national network."[243] The acronym, in PICO's third name change, now stands for "People Improving Communities through Organizing."[244]

PICO began quite modestly, as a California organization called the Oakland Training Institute (Oakland, California). It was founded in 1972 by two Jesuit priests, Father John Baumann, SJ and Father Jerry Helfrich, SJ.[245] Father Baumann, who was PICO's executive director until 2009, when he became PICO's Director of Special Projects,[246] got his start in community organizing in the summer of 1967, when he and

---

[242] A current listing of PICO affiliates can be found at the organization's website: www.piconetwork.org

[243] "About PICO,"PICO National Network website, www.piconetwork.org, Retrieved 8-21-09.]

[244] See, for example: www.facebook.com/pages/PICO-National-Network-People-Improving-Communities-Through-Organizing/54580146753?v=app_2347471856.

[245] Undated PICO informational material; Collection Description of the William F. Masterson Papers, 1960-2001, The Thomas and Dorothy Leavey Center for the Study of Los Angeles, 2009 Loyola Marymount.

[246] PICO News Release, "Fr John Baumann steps down after 36 years as Executive Director," PICO National Network, 12-22-08.

Helfrich were still seminarians and had been sent to attend the Urban Training Center in Chicago, "a program designed to educate the clergy and the religious in the skills of social involvement ." [247]

> Introduced to community organizing in 1967 when his Jesuit superiors sent him as a seminarian to work in Chicago's West Side neighborhoods, Father Baumann has been part of countless campaigns focusing on education reform, neighborhood safety, access to health care and the long-standing home foreclosure crisis....Father Baumann was ordained in 1969 and returned to Chicago for three years. In 1972, he was assigned to urban ministry in Oakland, Calif., where he opened the Oakland Training Institute, which helped develop community leaders. Eventually, the organization became the Pacific Institute for Community Organizing as it expanded across California. [248]

PICO's Alinskyian connections have always been in the open. "The organizers' training methods and strategies were — and still are — rooted in the teachings of Saul D. Alinsky, whose Back of the Yards Council in Chicago in the 1930s became the prototype for activist community organizations around the country," said the Rev. Mike Mandala, one of the original organizers from

---

[247] White House, President's Initiative on Race, Best Practices - Religious: Pacific Institute for Community Organization (PICO), clinton2.nara.gov/Initiatives/OneAmerica/Practices/09.pdf ; see also Donald C. Reitzes and Dietrich C. Reitzes, *The Alinsky Legacy: Alive and Kicking*, Jai Press (Greenwich, CT), 1987, pp 188-89.
[248] Mark Pattison, "USCCB official receives award from diocesan social action directors, *Catholic News Service*, 2-23-09.

Oakland.[249]

Specifically, Fathers Helfrich and Baumann were trained by Alinskyian organizer Thomas Gaudette. Gaudette and his wife had moved to Chicago during the 1950s, where they joined the Chicago branch of Pat and Patty Crowley's Christian Family Movement and discovered organizing through the Crowley's (and Alinsky's) great friend, Msgr. Jack Egan. Msgr. Egan introduced Gaudette to Alinsky as a potential organizer and Alinsky hired Gaudette in 1961 and personally trained him, overseeing Gaudette's organizing of the Northwest Community Organization (NCO) and, later, the Organization for a Better Austin (OBA), both in Chicago neighborhoods.[250]

Monsignor Egan credited Tom Gaudette with inspiring more community organizers than any other person, including — besides Fathers Baumann and Helfrich — Gail Cincotta of OBA who later founded the National Training and Information Center and another network of community organizations, National People's Action, with Shel Trapp.[251] Msgr. Egan saw to it that the influence included numerous churchmen:

> When Jack Egan brought Gaudette in to teach the seminarians how to make communities out of their blocks, Gaudette drilled them on two main techniques: listen to the community and confirm community involvement. The people of the

---

[249] Bob Schwartz, "Church Groups Prove They Can Fight City Hall," *LA Times*, 4-13-87.

[250] Gaudette Biography, Thomas and Dorothy Leavey Center for the Study of Los Angeles, 2009 Loyola Marymount.

[251] Sanford D. Horwitt, *Let Them Call Me Rebel*, Vintage Books, NY: 1989. Pp 544-545.

community had to venture their own capital, even if it wasn't money.

After Gaudette's sensitivization, Jack Macnamara and the other seminarians who surveyed their block/parishes were conditioned to *hear* the cry of the contract buyer when they got out on the streets. By Macnamara's lights, Jack Egan functioned as a CBL enabler "for activities, particularly organizing activities, which would never have happened if it wasn't for his initiative." Egan provided a base at Presentation [Church]. He reassured the Jesuit provincial of the legitimacy of the seminarians' activism.

....He [Egan] and Tom Gaudette had stood on their heads all day to convince some thirty Jesuit scholastics that community organization was fundamental to the common weal.[252]

PICO's "key intellectual strategist and visionary," Dr. José Carrasco, was another influential personality with ties to the Industrial Areas Foundation.[253]

EARLY YEARS

The 1972 Oakland Training Institute organized five neighborhood-based organizations, made up of individuals and families, in the Oakland, California area, among them the Oakland Community Organization (OCO), which was formally

---

[252] Margery Frisbie, *An Alley in Chicago: The Ministry of a City Priest*, 1991.
[253] Richard L. Wood, *Faith in Action: Religion, Race, and Democratic Organizing in America*, University of Chicago Press, 2002, p 292.

founded in 1977. [254]   Gaudette served as a consultant for OCO during these early years. [255]

When the Oakland Training Institute expanded to other parts of the state, Baumann renamed it the Pacific Institute for Community Organizations (PICO)[256] and shifted to a congregation-based (faith-based) and, therefore, *institution*-based model rather than individual membership, drawing from the experiences of COPS, an Industrial Areas Foundation in San Antonio. [257]   During the 1980s:

> The Pico network expanded greatly following its conversion from a neighborhood-based model to a more explicitly faith-based model and as a more religious cultural strategy took off. [258]

PICO's theory of organizing is that political power is generated from relationships, built on common values, among its member institutions, rather than from specific issues:

> When communities come in contact with one another and race and class begin to break down, and there's a common set of concerns about youth or after-school programming, quality of schools, access to health care – Republican or

---

[254] Annenberg Institute for School Reform, "Organized Communities, Stronger Schools: A preview of research findings," 2008.

[255] *The Alinsky Legacy*...p. 189.

[256] *The Alinsky Legacy*...p. 192.

[257] Heidi Swarts, *Organizing Urban America: Secular and Faith-Based Progressive Movements*, University of Minnesota Press, 2008, p. 144, discussing the PICO local affiliate, PACT.

[258] *Faith in Action*..., p 291.

> Democrat ideology really doesn't matter too
> much. Then it's a question of how do we fix this
> problem. [259]

What is not acknowledged, however, is that the
philosophical structure of such an organizational approach
determines the nature of which problems can be addressed by
the community organization – namely, those predetermined by
organizational leaders to be sufficiently "uncontroversial" or
"winnable" – as well as which solutions it can accept. Once
again, the organizers determine these matters, not the members
or the local leadership. [260]

PICO'S CALIFORNIA PROJECT

After little more than two decades of developing its local
bases, PICO was ready to begin expanding its influence. That
expansion began in 1994 with the establishment of a "state-wide
organizational effort in California with the goal of developing the
capacity of grassroots leaders to influence state policy in
Sacramento."[261]

The state-wide organization became a separate legal entity,
distinct from the PICO locals, in 1996, under the name of PICO
California Project (later shortened to simply PICO California).
Its first "action" was an education summit in San Jose described
as "mostly a show of force" but which may have had the desired
effect of influencing a "federal award of $25 million for school-

---

[259] *Organizing Urban America*...p 61, quoting an unidentified PICO organizer.
[260] See Chapter 38, section "Not Grassroots," for a more detailed discussion
of the organizers' control of the organization's agenda rather than local
control.
[261] Gordon Whitman, "Beyond Advocacy: The History and Vision of the
PICO Network," *Social Policy,* Winter 2006-7, p. 54.

to-career programs."[262] This didn't mean the locals worked on different issues. In fact, PICO's San Jose affiliate PACT worked for the same education reforms from the local perspective, demanding – and obtaining – new, small, "alternative" schools.

NEW VOICES CAMPAIGN

A concerted *national* thrust came in 2004, when PICO redefined its work as helping "low-income communities have an impact at the national level on such issues as immigration reform, health care, education, and rebuilding the Gulf Coast in the wake of Hurricane Katrina."[263] The initial goal was to build support for Congress' decision to fund Louisiana's Road Home plan.[264] PICO explained this move as:

> ....the need for community organizing to take federal power and policy more seriously. The staffing and communications infrastructure and organizational learning that PICO had developed to support national work helped the network respond to Katrina."[265]

---

[262] *Organizing Urban America*...p. 156. These federal "school-to-career" programs have been strongly promoted by other Alinskyian organizing networks, as well. For more information, see Chapter 10 on Education Reform.

[263] "New Voices Campaign," PICO National Network, www.piconetwork.org/newvoices.html, retrieved on 2008-08-22. *"Beyond Advocacy..."* p. 56 also identifies 2004 as the date when PICO began a "national strategy." Richard Wood, however, dates it from 2002, in "Higher Power: Strategic Capacity for State and National Organizing," *Community Organizing and Political Change in the City*, University of Kansas Press, 2007.

[264] *Beyond Advocacy...* p. 59.

[265] *Beyond Advocacy...* p. 58.

Scott Reed, on the PICO staff since 1977, and PICO's executive director since January 2009, [266] was a key architect of the New Voices Campaign, saying, "Our leaders increasingly understand the need for the federal level action..." [267]

As time passed, PICO has ventured into additional national issues, which will be discussed in greater detail below.

TRAINING

To develop its leadership, PICO conducts week-long national leadership development seminars several times a year through its National Leadership Development Seminars. These seminars teach the theory and practice of congregation-based organizing, [268] and local activists continue to be monitored closely by the hired organizer. [269]

Additional training is offered in various venues, such as the October 23-24, 2009 seminar titled "Community Organizing" at the Lane Center for Catholic Studies and Social Thought, which is part of the Jesuit University of San Francisco. [270]

There are interesting collaborations among PICO affiliates and some of the other community organizing networks. In 1985, PICO founded Organizing Leadership and Training Center (OLTC) "to develop new community organizations and support existing ones in New England states." [271] Today, OLTC has seven of its own, "distinct" local affiliates in Massachusetts and Vermont and four that are also members of the PICO

---

[266] Press release, "Fr. John Baumann steps down," PICO National Network, 12-22-08

[267] "Higher Ground..."

[268] PICO fact sheet, dated 9/95.

[269] *Organizing Urban America*...p. 147.

[270] "Not Neutral," *California Catholic Daily*, October 22, 2009.

[271] OLTC Mission Statement

network,[272] while the statewide PICO organization hyphenates its acronym with OLTC,[273] and another affiliate, the Greater Boston Interfaith Organization, is also a member of the IAF. OLTC affiliate Worcester Interfaith, with no formal ties to the IAF, trains its people using Greater Boston Interfaith Organization (IAF) resources. Then, there's OLTC affiliate Pioneer Valley Project, which is also part of the Inter-Valley Project (IVP) network. The relationships are complicated.

EDUCATION

As stated above, PICO's first "action" as a statewide political force in California was to hold an education summit in San Jose with the goal of influencing a "federal award of $25 million for school-to-career programs."[274]

Like all public meetings convened by Alinskyian organizations, this 1995 event was tightly controlled and highly ritualized. It included then US Education Secretary Richard Riley, "who encouraged PICO supporters gathered to push for federal education budgets that place a priority on school-to-work initiatives. By the time the two-hour session ended, California schools' superintendent Delaine Eastin pledged to stand 'shoulder to shoulder' with the churches in this fight."[275] Within the month, PICO was meeting with state officials and by the end of 1996, the National School-to-Work Office had

---

[272] Vermont Interfaith Action, Essex County Community Organization, United Interfaith Action of SE Massachusetts, and Brockton Interfaith Community

[273] www.mcan-oltc.org

[274] *Organizing Urban America*...p. 156.

[275] Gus Spohn, "A Less Visible Face of Church Activism: Believers Tackle Social Problems," American News Service, undated but accessed 7-24-97.

awarded California a School-to-Work implementation grant of
about $130 million over five years to develop the state's School-
to-Career system.[276]

PICO affiliates in California promoted this federal program
at the local level. The San Diego Organizing Project (SDOP),
for example, pushed a "Learn and Earn Campaign" as a
component of the school-to-career program.

> SDOP successfully lobbied the San Diego Unified
> School District Teachers Association and the San
> Diego County "School to Career Partnership" to
> integrate work experience with a regular
> academic curriculum. [277]

At around the same time, the Oakland PICO affiliate,
Oakland Community Organizations (OCO), was organizing for
education "reform" — the same "reform" programs as the other
Alinskyian networks have pushed around the country that, along
with desirable smaller classes, includes after-school programs,
school-to-career programs, and outcome-based pedagogy.

FORECLOSURE PROTECTION

At its 2008 November meeting in Washington, DC, PICO
affiliate leaders were trained to lobby Congress, the Treasury
Department, and the Federal Deposit Insurance Corporation as
part of an effort "to help people keep their homes when facing
foreclosure."[278] The larger effort was one of PICO's national

---

[276] School-to-Career in California Factsheet,
www.nww.org/qwbl/tools/caltoolkit/Factsheets/schooltocareerCA.pdf
[277] "Learn and Earn Apprenticeships Pay Dividends for San Diego Youth,"
Helping People Help Themselves, newsletter of the Friends of the Campaign for
Human Development, Fall 1997.
[278] Carolyn Said, "Faith-based effort to avert foreclosures," *San Francisco*

initiatives to coordinate a response to the housing crisis of 2008-2009, launching a "National Campaign to Stop Preventable Foreclosures."

As part of this campaign, PICO prepared a policy paper, "Too Big to Fail," which simplistically recommends turning "non-performing mortgages into performing mortgages."[279] It graphically describes lives broken by foreclosure and the nightmare of boarded-up neighborhoods, overrun with opportunistic gangs. PICO's solution is that would-be homeowners, seduced by unrealistic "mortgage products" offering borrowers low payments that eventually increase beyond their capacity to repay, simply require a mortgage "modification."

"The current system for turning non-performing mortgages – modifying loans on a case-by-case, individual basis," the PICO document says, "is not working." Using the experiences of Contra Costa County, California as its model, PICO believes a FDIC (Federal Deposit Insurance Corp) takeover of banks holding subprime adjustable rate mortgages will solve the problem. The FDIC then can offer mortgage holders the "modifications" – the loan adjustments – they need to stay in their homes. What could be easier? Problem solved.[280]

Sheila Bair, chair of the FDIC, has a similar perspective. She says:

> The continuing trend of unnecessary foreclosures imposes costs not only on borrowers and lenders,

Chronicle, www.sfgate.com/cgi-bin/article.cgi?file=/c/a/2008/10/28/MNI613P6T3.DTL, retrieved 2008-10-28.
[279] PICO National Network, "Too Big To Fail," October 2008, p. 3.
[280] "Too Big to Fail…" p 4; p. 15; p. 21

but also on entire communities...Foreclosures
may result in vacant homes that may invite crime
and create an appearance of market distress,
diminishing the market value of other nearby
properties.... The FDIC has strongly encouraged
loan holders and servicers to adopt systematic
approaches to loan modifications that result in
affordable loans that are sustainable over the long
term.[281]

Under this proposal, according to FDIC spokesman David
Barr, the FDIC would receive 80% of the loan's cash flow until
some unspecified level of payment is reached and then 60%
thereafter, causing one wag to comment:

If I were the buyer of these loans, this would be my
game plan:
1. Buy loans for 30 cents on the dollar
2. Network with Barney Frank
3. Network with Sheila Bair
4. Get some new housing stimulus passed to
"help distressed borrowers" REFI for 70-
80 cents on the dollar (if that doesn't work
then do a short sale, if that doesn't work
then foreclose)
5. Pocket the difference
6. Rinse, repeat.[282]

Yet, despite the patently untenable nature of the proposal,
clergy and congregants from more than 40 states were brought

---

[281] Statement of Sheila Bair, TARP Testimony to US House of
Representatives, November 19, 2008
[282] Short Sale Blogger.

together by the organizers of PICO to demand that the Department of Treasury require all banks getting a federal bailout package to adopt it.

"Remove the veil between the people of this nation and the people in authority. Pierce the veil of Secretary Paulson and Congress and move in their hearts today," one impassioned PICO-associated pastor prayed to the crowd's shouts of: "Wake up! Wake up, Secretary Paulson!" Activists then gave Paulson a letter signed by more than 500 clergy, asking him to end the foreclosure crisis according to PICO's determination.[283]

HEALTH INITIATIVE

As explained above, PICO has a long-standing interest in state-run health care programs, dating at least as far back as 1996 and its early PICO California Project activities. In 1996, PICO was consolidating power in metropolitan areas while exploring a state-wide effort to influence public policy on children's health in the state. California Children's Health Initiatives – programs to consolidate the health insurance programs of Medi-Cal, Healthy Families, and Healthy Kids into one package – are projects of both local PICO affiliates and PICO California.[284] PICO's contribution was not only to lend political support to these programs but to provide the programs with access to

---

[283] Ashley Gipson, "Faith communities rally for homeowners," *Baptist Standard,* November 28, 2008, quoting Marvin Webb, assistant pastor of Peniel Full Gospel Baptist Church in El Sobrante, CA.

[284] California Children's Health Initiatives (CHI) are in 30 counties across California, seeking to enroll "children into public programs, such as Medi-Cal and Healthy Families, as well as administering local Healthy Kids programs." www.cchi4kids.org/vision&mission.php. A list of CHI "partners:" www.cchi4kids.org/partners.php . For information about PACT's work in Santa Clara county, see: www.chikids.org .

members of the community through PICO churches. [285] In fact, "some congregations organize their own non-profit corporations to conduct social service programs."[286] By 2005, PICO California was a cosponsor of the California Healthy Kids Insurance Program. [287]

One ongoing criticism from watchdog groups has been that, as a political entity — one that includes many Catholic parishes with strong positions against abortion, contraception, and sexual activity outside of marriage — PICO-supported health care programs contain elements that accommodate, rather than address or correct, these social problems.

California Right to Life, for example, has described mobile health vans that travel around to different area dispensing health care services. As these vans are under the supervision of the County Public Health Department, they refer their clientele, including school children, to county agencies and non-profits such as Planned Parenthood that dispense birth control and abortion. Families without medical insurance are encouraged to sign up for Healthy Families, a California medical care program with options to cover such referrals.

The Contra Costa PICO affiliate was the primary promoter of the mobile medical van. In addition, PICO affiliates are the major source for lobbying in Sacramento for more school-based health clinics and government health care programs. Even more insidious, individuals have become "application assistants" operating within their church communities, trained and

---

[285] Camille Giglio, "Church-State Partnership: Solidarity for a New Morality," *San Francisco Faith*, January 2001.

[286] John Orr, "Faith-based Organizations and Welfare Reform: California Religious Community Capacity Study, Qualitative Findings and Conclusion," Center for Religion and Civic Culture, University of Southern California, November 2000, p. 6.

[287] California Bill Analysis, Bill No. AB 772, regarding California Healthy Kids Insurance Program, Senate Committee on Health, 6-29-05 (hearing).

authorized to sign up fellow congregants with Healthy
Families.[288]

> Churches that agree to become sites for
> recruiting applicants for the Healthy Families
> Insurance through the Parish Nurse Program
> receive $50 per successful application from the
> state Healthy Families fund…The applicant
> chooses one of five health insurance carriers all of
> whom provide elective abortion and family
> planning coverage. The Healthy Families
> enrollees may present themselves for health care
> to a large number of local, community agencies,
> health vans and clinics including Planned
> Parenthood.[289]

PICO has also used local initiatives to catapult its people into
advocacy for broader policy campaigns – for example, the Santa
Clara Children's Health Initiative "provided templates for
innovative state legislation."[290]

> PICO organizations have been working at the
> local and state level for the past decade to expand
> access to health coverage.[291]

More recently, several primary Alinskyian community

---

[288] California Right to Life, "Mobile SBCs/Parish Nurses," November 9, 2000
& "Healthy Families Program, Cont'd." November 22, 2000.
[289] Camille Giglio, "Church-State Partnership: Solidarity for a New Morality,"
San Francisco Faith, January 2001.
[290] *Beyond Advocacy…* p. 55.
[291] *Beyond Advocacy…* p. 59.

organizing networks across the country – with PICO being the most aggressive – actively campaigned for universal, national health care "reform," including abortion (and, as it turns out, mandatory contraceptive coverage) components. To this end, PICO and several other organizations ran a TV ad campaign in the summer of 2009 – one under the moniker of "People of Faith for Health Reform" – organizing nationwide prayer events, and recommending a "health care sermon weekend."

> The message, said PICO spokesman Gordon Whitman, is this: "Religious voters support health-care reform, and you can't take them for granted. We're not going to allow people who stand up for health reform to be attacked on religious grounds. If you are in a district or state that is culturally conservative, there is support for health reform." In August 2009, paid organizers will meet with pastors to help them organize their congregations, develop talking points for meetings with members of Congress and coordinate with other groups and individuals – religious and secular." [292]

Abortion provisions were no obstacle to PICO's support for nationalized healthcare reform. "To hold together their diverse memberships," the above PICO statement continues, "the coalitions are moving carefully around controversial issues. For example,… PICO [is] supporting the 'status quo' on abortion – neither requiring nor banning insurers from covering the procedure as long as federal funds are not used."

To demonstrate its support for universal, national healthcare,

---

[292] PICO National Network, "Pulling Together on Health Care," *Washington Post*, July 25, 2009

PICO joined an interfaith coalition called We Believe Together – Health Care for All, with over 40 religious bodies in its fold, including NETWORK, Catholics in Alliance for the Common Good and its partner organization Catholics United, Jim Wallis' *Sojourners Magazine*, and two other Alinskyian organizing networks – Gamaliel and Interfaith Worker Justice – and, not surprisingly, the Religious Coalition for Reproductive Choice.

Meanwhile, expansion of the federal State Children's Health Insurance Program (SCHIP) also received support from PICO. Expansion of SCHIP raised government insurance eligibility to include three-fifths of all American households, no longer functioning as a low-income safety net but as a program for low and middle-income families.[293] A precursor to a universal system under which states would receive "broad flexibility in its design so that it can be easily folded into . . . future program structures," health care "reform" is phased in by population groups.[294]

PICO therefore worked for universal healthcare both incrementally and directly. Yet another of its projects was Cover All Families, which was a campaign "to expand health coverage to uninsured children" and "to help organize the faith community to build bipartisan support for comprehensive healthcare reform."[295] It insisted that health care reform "needs to cover everyone, so that no person relies on an emergency room for their health care or delays treatment because they lack insurance or have been denied coverage."

To accomplish this, PICO trained its network "to hold public

---

[293] Diana Furchtgott-Roth, "SCHIP: The Creeping Nationalization of Health Care," *RealClearMarkets.com*, 1-29-09.
[294] Michael Franc, "SCHIP: A Step towards Socialism," *Human Events*, 07-27-07.
[295] www.piconetwork.org/coverallfamilies

events and communicate regularly with our Members of Congress about the need for comprehensive reform," and coordinated "with national religious denominations and faith-based organizations to bring a strong faith voice into the national healthcare debate…PICO is working to bring this unified voice into the debate."

HOUSING

PICO has not been engaged in the massive housing projects of other Alinskyian networks but some affiliates have certainly put their toes in the water.

PICO affiliate Oakland Community Organizations' (OCO) says one of its primary concerns is "to improve the quality and availability of affordable housing…under pressure from OCO, the city initiated an urban homestead program that brought the inventory of vacant HUD houses to almost zero."[296]

Decades later, in 2006, OCO formed a coalition with ACORN, labor groups, and others to push the Oakland Family Housing Act that, if passed, would have bizarrely mandated "that 20% of ALL new housing developments in Oakland are made accessible to custodians, teachers, hotel workers, firefighters and policemen." [297]

Another PICO affiliate, Contra Costa Interfaith Community Supporting Organization (CCICSO), worked with Catholic Charities on affordable housing through support of a 2002 legislative measure that brought $118 million in HUD funds to build on Catholic property. [298]

More generally, CCICSO backed the Contra Costa for Every

---

[296] "The Alinsky Legacy…," pp 190-1.
[297] www.oaklandfamilyhousingact.com ; the coalition is Oaklanders for Affordable Housing.
[298] The Oakland Diocese web page, Catholic Housing Initiative, has carried more information about this. The legislation was Proposition 46.

Generation, a local application of Smart Growth, a social engineering strategy to anticipate and respond to urban population development. [299] One of PICO's board members, [300] Alan B. Holloway, was also one of Contra Costa for Every Generation's "aging friendly advocates."[301] Holloway chairs the Y & H Soda Foundation board, [302] the foundation that, together with the John Muir/Mt. Diablo Community Health Fund created a Healthy Aging Initiative to create "sustainable, community-wide changes to address one of the most significant health challenges facing Contra Costa County: how to serve its rapidly aging population."[303]

Despite the rather idyllic picture painted by proponents of this massive social restructuring to accommodate the needs of aging citizens, critics fear a coercive underbelly to the program that would force all able-bodied elders to continue working. Grace Caliendo, CEO of the John Muir/Mt. Diablo Community Health Fund, is quoted as saying:

> There's this constant fear that the retirement of
> boomers is going to break the bank of Social
> Security and Medicare. Well, that's just not
> going to be true if we just keep on
> working....[we're]... not tired, a lot of us
> haven't had to do factory work or farm work or

---

[299] Camille Giglio, "Shelf Life: Smart Growth and Walnut Creek," October 31, 2005.

[300] www.piconetwork.org/about?id=0008

[301] www.foreverygeneration.org/docs/ foreverygeneration_people.pdf

[302] www.sodafoundation.org/browse/about/board_of_directors

[303] Muir/Mt. Diablo Community Health Fund website, www.johnmuirhealth.com/index.php/jmmdhs_benefits_fund_health_partn erships_healthy_aging.html

that kind of thing. I think society's going to need us.[304]

IMMIGRATION

A 2009 message from the PICO National Network on a community organizing discussion list says:

> For many years PICO has been working in immigrant and non-immigrant communities, building bridges and pushing for improvements to the immigration system. This has included work to promote citizenship, humane enforcement of existing immigration laws, and work to promote comprehensive immigration reform.
>
> Currently PICO affiliates across the country are promoting dialogues between communities, congregations, and with congressional representatives. PICO believes that the current immigration system that separates families and keeps millions in the shadows needs reform. For this reason, we are working in coordination with groups across the country to promote an immigration system that reflects our collective values as a nation.[305]

The message was to encourage supporters to join in a call to members of the US Congressional Hispanic Caucus, and discuss

---

[304] Diane Lily, "The Dance Continues," Vanishing Walnut Creek Blog, vanishingwalnutcreek.blogspot.com, 4-3-07.
[305] Discussion list for COMM-ORG, "PICO immigration reform organizing," issued by the PICO National Network to PICO supporters, 11-12-09.

"comprehensive immigration reform," as part of the National "Reform Immigration for America" campaign. The Principles of Immigration Reform articulated by the campaign include "helping all low-income Americans improve their job prospects and move up the economic ladder towards the American Dream," both native-born workers and immigrants, and "legalizing the status of undocumented immigrants working and living in the United States." [306]

Other actions of PICO make it clear that this approach to immigration reform is, indeed, organizational policy. For instance, Metro Organizations for People (MOP), PICO's Colorado affiliate, pushed legislation supporting comprehensive immigration reform in 2019. [307]

Six PICO affiliates [308] submitted a statement, signed by about 350 clergy, to the White House, the Department of Homeland Security, and key Congressional leaders, protesting immigration raids around the country.

The statement reads, in part: "We object to federal government action that has broken up families, left children abandoned, and traumatized whole communities. We should not need to shelter young children asking, "Where is my mother? Where is my father?" [309]

---

[306] National "Reform Immigration for America" campaign, salsa.wiredforchange.com

[307] PICO news release, "Over 1,000 turn out in Denver for Comprehensive Immigration Reform," 1-15-10.

[308] United Interfaith Action (UIA, New Bedford, MA); Congregations Building Community (CBC, Greeley, CO); Contra Costa Interfaith Supporting Community Organization (CCISCO); People Acting in Community Together (PACT, San Jose, CA); Peninsula Interfaith Action (PIA, San Mateo County, CA); Oakland Community Organizations (OCO)

[309] PICO National Network, CCISCO *Immigration Update 507*, undated but the Statement was issued in May 2007.

Related to its policies on immigration, PICO's health care project, Cover All Families, "to expand health coverage to uninsured children," includes undocumented workers. "Reform needs to *cover everyone*, so that no person relies on an emergency room for their health care or delays treatment because they lack insurance or have been denied coverage." [emphasis in the original] [310]

---

[310] www.coverallfamilies.org ; see Sue Dremann, "Faith groups take up immigration, health issues: Forum Saturday will bring together local elected officials, advocates for change," *Palo Alto Weekly*, 7-17-09.

6. Gamaliel

BACKGROUND

The Gamaliel Foundation traces its origins to 1968, when it was founded "to support the Contract Buyers League, an African American organization fighting to protect homeowners on Chicago's Westside who organizers believed had been discriminated against by banks and saving and loan institutions."[311]

The exact dates of its first years are somewhat sketchy. Greg Galluzo, Gamaliel's founder and executive director, writes that he and Mary Gonzalez, a Chicago Latino activist who became his wife, created the Chicago-based United Neighborhood Organization (UNO) in 1980, bringing the Alinsky-trained Jerry Kellman to help them "become better organizers" two years later. Around the same time, he says, they created the Gamaliel Foundation.[312]

The UNO remembers its founding a bit differently: "The United Neighborhood Organization (UNO) was established by a group of community leaders and local Priests (sic) in 1984. Modeled on the Saul Alinsky style of community organizing, we sought to build grass-roots leadership within Chicago's Hispanic neighborhoods to organize for power and address local issues such as prevalent street violence and overcrowding in schools."[313]

Whatever the exact dates, Galluzo, who had been a Jesuit

---

[311] www.gamaliel.org/Foundation/history.htm
[312] Gregory Galluzo, "Gamaliel and the Barack Obama Connection," from The Gamaliel Foundation website.
[313] UNO website, www.uno-online.org, "About" section.

priest, was trained by and organized under Saul Alinsky:[314]

> …Greg Galluzzo and his wife Mary Gonzalez, took over the Gamaliel Foundation after breaking with the *Industrial Areas Foundation* (IAF), the organization founded by Saul Alinsky. Gamaliel's leadership system was built on notes obtained from the IAF. They eventually modified the system, but to my knowledge they have never credited the IAF even for the initial iteration of the so-called Gamaliel model.[315]

The Foundation was reorganized and became distinctively faith-based in 1986 under Galluzo's leadership, when he became its founding executive director.[316] For his wife's part, Gonzalez directed Ntosake, a Gamaliel leadership training program for women, and the Metropolitan Alliance of Congregations, the Gamaliel coalition of its Chicago-based affiliates.[317] Today, she

---

[314] Robert Kleidman, associate professor for the department of Sociology, Cleveland State University, "Community Organizing: A View from the Bottom Up," 1994 – prepared under a grant from the Aspen Institute; Heidi Swarts, *Organizing Urban America…,* also identifies Galluzzo as a former Jesuit priest – p 236, FN 9.

[315] Rey Lopez-Calderon, "Walking the Edge of Immorality: It's Time for Community Organizers to Expose Corruption Within Our Own Ranks," Cockroach People: Rants and ruminations by a classical liberal with radical Chicano tendencies [Blog: cockroachpeople.com/?p=702], 10-8-09. Lopez-Calderon was an organizer for Gamaliel from "the late 1990s up until 2001.")

[316] As of January, 2011, Gamaliel's executive director is Ana Garcia-Ashley. Gamaliel Press Release, "At 25-Year Mark, Gamaliel Directorship Passes to Woman of Color," 1-5-11.

[317] "The Gamaliel Foundation," 4-page information material about the Foundation, prepared by the Gamaliel Foundation, undated; An Institute for Woman's Policy Research publication, Research-in-Brief (April 2006) says that Notosake is a South African word meaning "she who walks with lions and carries her own things."

is the California Director for the Foundation.[318]

In 2011, Ana Garcia Ashley replaced Galluzzo as Gamaliel's executive director. She has organized with the group for quite some time, having led the Wisconsin local MICAH in the early 90s and becoming a regional director a few years later.[319] Ashley has also acted as co-director of Gamaliel's immigration campaign, Civil Rights of Immigrants (CRI).[320] Galluzzo remains very much in the picture, listed as a Senior Organizer among the Gamaliel staff.[321]

THE GAMALIEL PLATFORM

Gamaliel is very open about its ambition to "[b]uild and mobilize a constituency for progressive change in the United States."[322] Its "Faith and Democracy Platform" suggests what "progressive change" might entail:

> The Gamaliel Foundation is an organizing institute that brings together communities of people living out our faith and values to bring about justice and collectively transform our society. ...Confronting what divides us is deeply

---

[318] www.gamaliel.org/DIRECTORY/marybio.htm   The Gamaliel Bio lists her as the California Director; other sources give her the title of "Western Territory" or "Western Region" Director.

[319] Tom Tolan, "Franklin Resident amped up to head Gamaliel Foundation," *Milwaukee, Wisconsin Journal Sentinel*, JSOnline, 2-27-11.

[320] National Staff: www.gamaliel.org/Contact/Directory/NationalStaff.aspx (accessed 4-15-11); also Media/Communications and NLA," (National Leadership Assembly, Gamaliel), 9-1-03.

[321] National Staff: www.gamaliel.org/Contact/Directory/NationalStaff.aspx (accessed 4-15-11).

[322] A Gamaliel Foundation Job Description, 10-1-09.

> spiritual and requires humility and openness to
> transformation. This is also deeply political
> because civilizations and societies are structured
> around how they answer this question. Spiritual
> transformation and societal transformation are
> linked. As people of faith, we proclaim that all
> our fates are linked; we are connected and that
> love is at the center. ... The transformation of the
> soul of our country, our democracy, is both a
> political project and a spiritual project. It requires
> a body of people willing to live, to act, and to
> project a new way of being. Our faith is a path to
> a new way of being: spiritually and politically.
> Gamaliel exists to effect the systemic changes
> necessary to advance the values we have claimed,
> and to that end, to form organizations that
> empower ordinary people to effectively
> participate in the political, environmental, social
> and economic decisions affecting their lives.[323]

The political and spiritual transformations to which Gamaliel and its members commit in the Platform are not defined. One might dismiss this as self-inflating bombast except that if the Foundation merely sought additional health care or welfare government programs, it would not require "systemic change" and "a new way of being" to implement them.

However, the programs to which the Platform refers do, indeed, create "systemic change." The Gamaliel Foundation's proposed health care reform insists that "each person has an equal right to quality health care," which is quite a different matter than the traditional belief that society has a humanitarian

---

[323] Gamaliel Foundation's "Faith and Democracy Platform," www.gamaliel.org/platform.htm.

obligation to care for its sick. Government – and a sizeable portion of the US economy – must be structured (or restructured) if it is to guarantee each citizen his new "rights."

Perhaps anticipating the religious community's objections to such restructuring, and its consequences for them, the Platform then uses the liberationist trick of quoting the scripture: "Then Jesus called the twelve together and gave them power and authority over all demons and to cure diseases, and he sent them out to proclaim the kingdom of God and to heal" (Luke 9:1-2), and then twists the meaning to its own purposes. This passage, the reader is told, demonstrates that "health care is a God-given right" and, therefore, the evangelical work of religious institutions is to support the Gamaliel Platform of engaging "in strategic statewide and national campaigns to achieve universal access to affordable, quality health care for all residents of the United States."

Nor does this proposed health care reform exist in isolation. The Platform continues that it is to be achieved, hand in glove, with comprehensive immigration reform, assuring undocumented workers full participation "in a country they have helped to build."

Furthermore, "every family deserves to live in an 'opportunity community,' defined as a community that includes both good jobs and good schools... .fair share housing (that assures government supported low income housing isn't concentrated in poor neighborhoods) ....transportation systems that provide equal access for all members of the community, as well as sustain and support the whole creation....workforce development agreements with state transportation departments and other public entities." The scope of federal government control proposed here requires nothing less than a complete overhaul of governance as we know it. That is what is meant by "systemic change."

Gamaliel is correct that this would require "a new way of being: spiritually and politically." Traditional Judeo-Christian thought understands "doing good," such as helping the sick, as a moral obligation. Fulfillment of moral obligations is an act of free-will and therefore obligations that ought to be observed, can also be ignored. The habitual doer of good is virtuous; the habitual abstainer from good is peccant…and this leaves the needy dependent upon the virtue of others, which may be wanting.

If, however, the goods of life are the "right" of everyone to possess rather than an obligation on the more fortunate to help the less fortunate, individuals are morally justified in demanding that their "rights" be provided and must do whatever is necessary to secure them. Thinking along this vein, the secular Alinskyian organizing mind cannot wait for someone to "do good." Rather, society must be organized to bestow goods on everyone, without reference to the virtue of anyone dispensing them. Small surprise that "goods" gathered irrespectively of moral good – and systems bestowing them amorally – consistently fall far short of their promise.

HEALTH CARE "REFORM"

As indicated above, one of the Gamaliel network's major thrusts has been health care "reform." Shortly after the 2008 US presidential elections, its website announced: "Barack H. Obama, former GAMALIEL ORGANIZER, is the 44th President of the United States!" (emphasis in the original) along with the declaration that on June 22-25, 2009, it had bussed in hundreds of clergy and leaders from across the country to Washington DC for visits to congressional representatives to discuss health care. "The Gamaliel National Clergy Caucus is leading Gamaliel's newest national issue: Health Care. They invite you and your spiritual community to discuss and then act on their latest theological statement."[324]

To this end, Gamaliel joined the Health Care for America Now coalition that includes several other Alinskyian organizing networks such as ACORN, as well as some pro-abortion groups, including the Religious Coalition for Reproductive Choice and Planned Parenthood Federation of America. Because of Gamaliel's ties to these groups, with their emphatic, pro-abortion position, the Catholic Diocese of Green Bay under Bishop David Ricken threatened to sever ties with the national and affiliate groups in 2010.[325] The bishop's concerns were:

- No bishop or a leader of another faith can adequately oversee a given political position or an association that WISDOM or Gamaliel might engage in. Last fall's confusion over Health Care for America Now (HCAN) is a recent example.
- In a similar vein, it's not reasonable to expect other organizations, such as WISDOM or Gamaliel, to clear a political position with a bishop or church leader.
- Political positions and activities of WISDOM and Gamaliel won't always coincide with the church's positions and guidelines set forth by the *U.S. Conference of Catholic Bishops* (USCCB).
- The Catholic Church in Wisconsin and in the United States has an established network of resources. The *Wisconsin Catholic Conference* and the USCCB identify and work on political positions and nonpartisan political

---

[324] www.gamaliel.org, since changed. Emphasis was in the original.
[325] J.E. Espino, "Green Bay Catholic Diocese Worries about Interfaith Groups' Advocacy," *Green Bay Press-Gazette*, 2-24-10.

activity. Gamaliel, WISDOM, and their affiliates create confusion when their position differs from that of the church.[326]

Gamaliel was also a key player of the *We Believe Together - Health Care for All* coalition that included the PICO National Network, Sojourners, and Catholics in Alliance for the Common Good. This particular coalition held a *40 Days for Health Reform* campaign to mobilize religious institutions around the issue. Within the coalition's various networks, the campaign sponsored a highly publicized conference call between President Obama and the "people of faith" to discuss health care reform. It ran a nationwide TV ad featuring clergy in support of proposed health care reform legislation and disseminated material with misapplied scripture verses, such as the Matthew 25's warning that people will "be judged by how they treat the least of these," implying there was a spiritual mandate for the legislation: "Healing is God's desire for every person because everyone is created in the divine image."[327] How it follows from this that God has suddenly, after 2000 years, commanded socialized health care was never explained. Clearly, this is an abuse of religious sensibilities to force people into accepting the political position currently in fashion.

SMART GROWTH

In 1996, the Gamaliel network adopted what it dubbed

---

[326] Renae Bauer, "Bishop Ricken Meets with Catholic Core Members of JOSHUA and ESTHER," The Compass, Diocesan newspaper for the Catholic Diocese of Green Bay, Wisconsin, 3-25-10.

[327] Sojourners' Health Care Toolkit, www.sojo.net/action/alerts/health_care_toolkit.pdf. For more information about the Alinskyian organization's role in pushing US health care reform legislation, see chapter 14.

"progressive regionalism" as a basic organizing strategy.[328] Progressive regionalism is a form of urban development – one that is far more encompassing than earlier efforts:

> Progressive regionalism advocates far-reaching, comprehensive smart growth measures including urban growth boundaries, which either prohibit development outside a defined perimeter or deny subsidies such as water and sewer to developers who wish to create new urbanized areas. Without such subsidies, new developments are typically not profitable. Progressive regionalists link this fact to the equity argument that older cities and suburbs, through the tax dollars of their residents, have been required to subsidize the new growth that has contributed greatly to their decline. Less comprehensive smart growth measures include redirecting federal and state funds away from new highways and other projects that encourage outmigration, and toward repair and maintenance of older infrastructure in the core (cities and inner suburbs), the cleanup of 'brownfields' - older industrial and commercial sites that are often highly polluted - etc. [329]

---

[328] "Community Organizing: A View …"

[329] "Community Organizing: A View from the Bottom Up …" The Global ARC (see FN 18) explains: "The term *progressive* is used in an increasingly wide range of academic, grassroots, institutional, policy and planning contexts. In addition to progressive planning one can find diverse calls for progressive regionalism, progressive globalization, progressive governance, progressive communications, progressive cities, and progressive networks. Planning has its roots in progressive ideas. …Progressive planning combines critical theory, practical know how, organizing skills, vision and action in

Gamaliel's promotion of Smart Growth urban planning was considered one of its "guiding orientations" and specifically developed what it called "regional equity organizing (REO)" to

> ….build a "metropolitan majority" in the declining and at-risk communities, to promote policies that slow or stop sprawl, create reinvestment in the core, and provide transportation to and housing in affluent suburbs for some poor people. These policies typically require action at regional and state levels. REO's vision is an environmentally sustainable region, preserving its natural and architectural heritage in a compact urban core, with increasing economic and racial integration and equality. [330]

Gamaliel's commitment to progressive regionalism began when its Minneapolis affiliate, ISAIAH, began collaborating with Minnesota State Representative Myron Orfield, who remains a "strategic partner" of Gamaliel, on the problem of neighborhood deterioration and specifically the number of contaminated "brownfield" sites in the Minneapolis-St. Paul area. With Orfield's assistance, "leaders in ISAIAH member congregations organized the passage of a bill that committed $68 million toward the clean-up of Minnesota's brownfields."[331]

The comprehensive aspect of "progressive regionalism" is

---

community-based efforts to eradicate poverty, social injustice, and unhealthy living conditions. Progressive imaginations create actionable visions of alternative development for the good society."

[330] Robert Kleidman, "Community Organizing and Regionalism," *City and Community* 3:403-421, 2004.

[331] ISAIAH informational webpage: "What is Isaiah?" www.gamaliel.org/isaiah/whoweare/whatisisaiah.htm.

truly breath-taking. It includes, but isn't limited to, addressing climate change, overseeing urban design, community development, economic development, food planning, global planning, housing, infrastructure, and public health.[332]

How it plays out on the local level can be seen in the work of the Gamaliel affiliate of St. Louis, Metropolitan Congregations United for St. Louis (MCU). While MCU "leadership" – that is, persons chosen from among MCU member institutions – are trained to conduct one-on-one interviews to develop support for MCU initiatives, the Gamaliel Foundation…

> …has an ongoing consulting relationship with several "Strategic Partners" who have guided its "metropolitan analysis" and who consult with Gamaliel locals and the national staff. Because Gamaliel locals such as MCU place such emphasis on regional policy reform, they see town meetings and other efforts to educate members, the public, and authorities about their proposed policies as essential. [333]

One cannot read the above without observing that the "town hall meeting," designed as a forum for citizens to express their opinions to public officials, becomes an "educational" vehicle in the hands of the Alinskyian organizers to educate their own members, whose opinions will be, presumable, the same as Gamaliel's, once those opinions are properly formed.

---

[332] The Global ARC (Action Research Center), handout: "Progressive Community-Based Planning: A Sustainability Framework." The Global ARC is "a network of individuals and organizations committed to progressive sustainable development."
[333] *"Organizing Urban America…,"* p 114-5.

In this case, the experts guiding MCU's — that is, Gamaliel's — urban policies were David Rusk and Myron Orfield,[334] apologists for Smart Growth. "MCU's grassroots leaders were jolted by this analysis," during a 1996 series of educational forums taught by Rusk and Orfield. According to one participant, the workshops "opened our eyes." "MCU framed the issue" of urban sprawl "positively as 'smart growth'" and formed the Smart Growth Alliance to campaign for urban growth boundaries.[335] MCU understood its victory in terms of getting St. Louis citizens and their churches engaged in local politics, of drawing them into the action, and getting them to understand "these issues as manifestations of a larger problem,"[336] as seen through the Gamaliel lens.

IMMIGRATION

In September 2008, Gamaliel joined a network of faith-based groups in a campaign to demand "immigration reform." The campaign included an 18-city "Tour of the Faithful," during which the network held "immigration vigils," press conferences, educational workshops, and marches, hoping to influence the US presidential candidates into support of legalization of illegal immigrants.

Rev. Samuel Rodriguez, president of the National Hispanic Christian Leadership Conference, which is part of this network, characterized any solution other than legalization of illegal immigrants as "xenophobic" and "nativist." Presumably, the other organizations within the network hold similar views.

After the 2009 presidential election, these same faith-based

---

[334] David Rusk describes their position as "National Strategic Partners of the Gamaliel network," www.gamaliel.org/DavidRusk/DavidRuskMission.htm
[335] *"Organizing Urban America…,"* p 120.
[336] *"Organizing Urban America…,"* p 124.

groups held a national teleconference to urge an end to Immigration and Customs Enforcement (ICE) operations throughout the country. Cardinal Roger Mahony, Archbishop of Los Angeles, speaking during the teleconference, advised president-elect Obama not to repeat the mistake of the 1986 amnesty bill, which he felt was too limited. "They said they'd get to the other pieces later, and they never did. By doing it piecemeal, we run the risk of never getting it done."

"Comprehensive" immigration reform seeks legal status for any worker in the United States, along with due process rights, an end to household and workplace raids, improved treatment of minors and families picked up for immigration violations, and a better process for addressing backlogs of people waiting to enter the country legally. The Gamaliel CRI – Civil Rights of Immigrants – project backed, for instance, the "Solve Act," national legislation introduced in 2004 to address exactly these points. Gamaliel "Rolling Thunder" meetings were held in ten states to drum up support and enthusiasm for the legislation, particularly among Gamaliel affiliates' member congregations.[337]

While the legislation wasn't passed, the struggle for similar reform continues. Unfortunately, no proposed bills have yet tackled the fundamental problem of how a sovereign state controls its borders. Are they to be "open," that is, essentially unregulated? Is there any limitation placed on the number of immigrants a sovereign state must accommodate? If so, how are new immigrants awarded legal status? How are criminals kept out? How does the country provide adequately for the needs of these workers? As one journalist expressed it, comprehensive immigration reform doesn't address "the legality or individual

---

[337] Gamaliel Foundation, "The Time Has Come for Comprehensive Immigration Reform!!!!" CRI Newsletter, 12-1-04.

rights of immigrants; it instead discusses the community-level impact of a broken immigration system."[338] They are all important questions, nevertheless.

Another unaddressed problem is the manner in which this comprehensive reform movement is being spread. Does sponsorship of "faith-based" groups in a "Tour of the Faithful" mean the comprehensive reform movement is godly, righteous, and prophetic while any criticism of the reform – such as suggesting it doesn't reform *enough* – is unfaithful, probably sinful, and, yes, xenophobic, to boot? That does seem to be the intended implication.

JOBS NOW CAMPAIGN

Federal job programs are another concern of the Gamaliel Foundation. Gamaliel created the Transportation Equity Network (TEN) [339] and, in August 2007, Gamaliel, Smart Growth America, and TEN published a study, "The Road to Jobs: Patterns of Employment in the Construction Industry in Eighteen Metropolitan Areas," as the basis of a JOBS NOW campaign. [340] The JOBS NOW Campaign seeks "thousands of high paying jobs for low-income people, minorities, women, and ex-offenders through workforce development agreements and policies."[341]

---

[338] Corine Hegland, *National Journal*, 12-13-08
[339] "TEN is a project of the Gamaliel Foundation, a faith-based organization with regional affiliates around the United States, and Smart Growth America." TEN's affiliates include not only various Gamaliel affiliates but several DART and IAF affiliates as well, along with a host of independent organizing efforts.
www.transportationequity.org/index.php?option=com_content&view=article&id=13&Itemid=30.
[340] www.transportationequity.org
[341] www.gamaliel.org/issues/issuework/jobsnow.htm

To accomplish this, TEN and its legislative backers piggy-backed an amendment onto the 2005 Safe Accountable Flexible and Efficient Transportation Equity Act-A Legacy for Users (SAFETEA-LU), a $286 billion federal appropriation bill for highways and public transit). This amendment mandated that 30% of highway-project jobs be filled by the above-mentioned groups. In truth, the total number of jobs remained the same but employed different populations.

7. Other Alinskyian Organizing Networks

One of the overwhelming aspects of studying Alinskyian organizing is the degree to which it has replicated and spread. Over the years, numerous trained individuals have felt they could use aspects of Alinsky's methodology while bringing their own perspectives to the mix.

> Even activists such as Heather Booth and Shel Trapp, who never or only briefly met Alinsky, have been touched by his philosophy. Local leadership, confrontational tactics, personalizing the issue — all well-recognized and widely practiced tenets taught by Booth and Trapp at their training schools in Chicago — were espoused for the first time in *Reveille for Radicals* and *Rules for Radicals*, the two primers Alinsky wrote. And through it all, he developed almost a personality cult of admirers, young and old, galvanized by his persona: the caustic, acerbic and witty University of Chicago graduate who scored scholars and academicians and struck a pose of street-smart tough.[342]

The groups considered below owe more than a passing debt of gratitude to Alinsky. Like the major Alinskyian organizing networks – the IAF, PICO, Gamaliel, and ACORN – these have similar features that make them problematic for religious institutions, whether as members or as funding sources.

---

[342] Ben Joravsky, "Community organizing: Alinsky's legacy," *Illinois Issues*, January 1988.

DART (DIRECT ACTION AND RESEARCH TRAINING CENTER)

The Direct Action and Research Training Center – DART – was founded by John Calkins, its current executive director. His introduction to the world of community organizing came in 1968, while a graduate student at the University of Wisconsin. Calkins was recruited to participate in a protest march over welfare cuts, invited by Father James Groppi, an outspoken civil rights advocate who served as advisor to the Milwaukee chapter of the National Association for the Advancement of Colored People (NAACP). [343] Thanks to the interest this experience sparked, Calkins became increasingly engaged in organizing and eventually head organizer of the Wisconsin Welfare Rights Organization (WWRO), where he worked until 1974. [344]

In 1977, Herb White, a clergyman who had worked with, and was trained by, Saul Alinsky in Rochester, New York hired Calkins to organize senior citizens in Miami. [345] Racial turmoil was so intense in the city during the next several years, however, that his Concerned Seniors of Dade sponsored a second organization, People United to Lead the Struggle for

---

[343] Background material is from the DART Center website unless otherwise noted [www.thedartcenter.org].

[344] Wikipedia: en.wikipedia.org/wiki/James Groppi; *Wisconsin Magazine of History*: Volume 90, number 4, summer 2007; Groppi left the priesthood in 1976, married and had three children.

[345] Mark G. Hanna, Buddy Robinson, *Strategies for community empowerment: direct-action and transformative approaches to social change practice*, Mellen, 1994. White went on to the Philippines to organize "priests, sisters, ministers and young activists" working in the Manila slums, forming the Philippine Ecumenical Committee for Community Organization (PECCO) according to the "Alinsky method." More information about White's work in Asia can be read at: Leaders and Organizers of Community Organization in Asia (LOCOA) website: www.locoa.net/home; also, Jennifer Conroy Franco, *Elections and Democratization in the Philippines*, Routledge, 2001, p 119.

Equality (PULSE), to address police brutality against African-Americans.

Calkins saw "the state of Florida as grounds for a network of local community organizations" and founded the DART Center in 1980 to coordinate it. The Center incorporated in 1982 and expanded its activities into other states.

DART materials emphasize the training in community organizing it provides. The Center offers two five-day orientation workshops, an annual Clergy Conference, an Advanced Leader Training Institute, 4-month paid "field schools," and regular local training workshops.

In 2001, DART established the DART Organizers Institute "to identify and train professional community organizers. DART ultimately adds the Organizers Institute as a major element in its annual strategic plan to include a seven month national recruitment search, a two month interview process, and a four month intensive initial training followed by two years of on-going advanced training and professional organizer development."

As with the other Alinskyian organizing networks, DART affiliates confront government and agency officials in public rallies called Nehemiah Actions,[346] which attempt to force commitments to the DART agenda.[347]

> The Action Meeting [another term for a Nehemiah Action] is a grand exercise of organized people power where city officials and decision-makers are asked point-blank, yes or no, whether they will carry out the solutions

---

[346] Similar to the IAF's accountability assemblies.
[347] Eileen Soler, "Church activists are tackling social issues," The Miami Herald, 4-18-10.

proposed. When faced with hundreds and
sometimes thousands of determined people and a
well-researched, reasonable solution to a specific
issue, few officials can say no![348]

Like other Alinskyian networks, DART has developed
regional[349] and national networking, with its local affiliates
pushing the same statist solutions to current problems. The
education "reform" DART affiliates espouse is the same
nationally-driven outcome-based education[350] promoted by the
other Alinskyian networks. For example, Louisville,
Kentucky's CLOUT[351] pushed Direct Instruction reading
curriculum in its local public schools, as did Tampa, Florida's
HOPE[352] and Toledo, Ohio's TUSA. [353] The DART website
says, in a section about the organization's accomplishments,
"First and foremost, many DART organizations have succeeded
in implementing and expanding effective reading curriculum in
our public schools such as Direct Instruction (DI)."

---

[348] Michael John Kelley, "Social Justice," The Sonikcycle Syndicate weblog,
11-20-06.

[349] DART Ohio, for example, "is a coalition of four grassroots community
organizations," namely BREAD – Columbus, OH; LEAD – Dayton, OH;
JAM – Springfield, OH; and TUSA – Toledo, OH.
www.toledoans.us/dart.shtml

[350] "Outcome-based-education" (OBE) or "mastery" education goes by many
names and the programs which operate according to its philosophy are legion
– and also go by many different names. "OBE became so controversial by
the mid-1990s that the term was dropped but the OBE cycle for in-school
behavior modification has continued under other names." (John A. Stromer,
None Dare Call it Education," Liberty Bell Press, 1998, p 136.) There is
more detailed discussion about OBE in chapter 10 on Education Reform.

[351] CLOUT - Citizens of Louisville Organized and United Together

[352] HOPE - Hillsborough Organization for Progress & Equality

[353] TUSA - Toledoans United for Social Action

DART argues that Direct Instruction accelerates learning and has improved reading skills for at-risk students in low performing public schools. Critics of Direct Instruction, on the other hand, call it "Skinnerian." Despite the claim of being a "phonics-based reading program," research educators call it another term for "mastery learning" or "outcome-based education."[354] One direct instruction program, Success for All, was reviewed and drew the following comments: "The prevailing criticism of Success for All is that it is designed to produce higher scores on a couple of tests chosen by Slavin [its creator], for which the control-group schools don't train their students; the gains it produces, according to critics, are substantially limited to the first year of the program."[355]

The article goes on to describe a "relentlessly" structured classroom, marked by loud, mindless drills and a tightly controlled, "teacher-proof" curriculum. "'If you work right, you'll earn points for your team! You clear?' Twenty voices call out, 'Yes!'" Critics believe such a system is devoid of thought process and is designed to produce uniform and conformist people.

TUSA has pushed another educational program of concern, Positive Behavior Support (PBS). PBS is "a research-based

---

[354] Charlotte Thomson Iserbyt, *The Deliberate Dumbing of America: A Chronological Paper Trail,* Conscience Press, 1999, p 228. The thesis of Iserbyt and other educational researchers who blew the whistle on outcome based education (OBE) in the 1990s is that this particularly pedagogy is patterned after Soviet educational theories and deliberately designed to produce compliant citizens with a merely functional level of literacy. Iserbyt, who was Senior Policy Advisor in the Office of Educational Research and Improvement, provides an enormous volume of evidence to support this contention. See chapter 10 on education reform.

[355] Nicholas Leman," Ready, READ!" *Atlantic Monthly,* November 1998, quoted in *The Deliberate Dumbing of America...* p 435.

discipline program" that employs behavior modification techniques to produce desired behaviors in school children. Pinellas County's FAST[356] has fought for a specific PBS program, the "Foundations/CHAMPS model of proactive, instructional, and positive behavior management."

While behavior modification has its place when used – with the permission of parents who are given adequate prior information about it – to control severely troubled children, school-wide applications of these programs are disturbingly inappropriate.

In other areas, DART's work is to engage the local community in order to advance a national purpose. Louisville, Kentucky's CLOUT "won a commitment" from state and local health officials "to form a task force and develop a pilot project to enroll 6,000 more children in Medicaid & KCHIP (Kentucky Child Health Insurance Program)" in 2008. [357] Tallahassee, Florida's TEAM[358] affiliate pushed to reinstate $1.2 million for Bond Neighborhood Health Centers. Daytona Beach, Florida's FAITH[359] helped "thousands of people without healthcare" to sign up for the Hospital's indigent care program."

As a final thought, John Calkins is on the Board of Directors of the Organizer's Forum[360] and DART's own Board includes Bruce Hanson, retired after 29 years with the Center for

---

[356] FAST - Faith and Action for Strength Together
[357] DART website, "Accomplishments," www.thedartcenter.org/accomplishments.html. Further mention of DART "accomplishments" to provide healthcare coverage come from here.
[358] TEAM - Tallahassee Equality Action Ministry
[359] FAITH - Fighting Against Injustice and Toward Harmony
[360] The Organizers' Forum Board of Directors, www.organizersforum.org/index.php?id=352

Community Change,[361] giving DART ties to the broader community of Alinskyian organizing.

MIDWEST ACADEMY, CITIZEN ACTION PROGRAM, AND USACTION

The Midwest Academy was founded by Heather Tobis Booth, an activist from Chicago with roots in the abortion "rights" movement where, under the code name "Jane," she helped women in the mid 1960s procure illegal abortions.

> I would counsel the women, preparing them for the abortion and doing follow-up with them and with the doctor afterward. Many of the women who called me were students. Some were housewives. At least a couple of women were related to the Chicago police. It made me believe that the police department knew about it, and might even be referring people. The law did not change until 1973, and until then abortion was illegal; I didn't want to go to jail. I was willing to take the risks because I thought I was fulfilling the Golden Rule.... Jane ultimately served over 10,000 women before *Roe v. Wade* made abortion legal in 1973.[362]

Heather met her husband Paul Booth in 1966 at the University of Chicago, where she was studying. Paul, National Secretary of the Chicago-based Students for a Democratic

---

[361] www.thedartcenter.org/staff.html;
kybele2010.wikispaces.com/Who+Are+We
[362] Heather Booth, Statement, Jewish Women's Archive:
jwa.org/feminism/_html/JWA004.htm

Society (SDS) at the time, had come to the campus to organize anti-war protests.[363] For her part, Heather was an extraordinarily energetic activist, chairing the university's leftist Student Political Action Committee in its anti-war work and founding a women's "consciousness-raising" group. They admired each other's work and married the following year.[364]

The Booths were committed socialists, coauthoring a pamphlet titled *Socialism and the Coming Decade* with SDS field secretary Steve Max and community organizer Harry Boyte.[365] The pamphlet is:

> ...all about long-term strategy, realistic short-term objectives, and the deep-down social change that only patient community organizing can bring. For all that, the program itself remains radical, with clear support for the Vietnamese communists and a guaranteed annual income for all Americans among its positions, for example. Even so, the SDSers behind "*Socialism and the Coming Decade*" counsel patience... in these non-revolutionary times, we're told, "a conscious organization of socialists" needs to found and guide community organizations among the working class. These neighborhood groups can mobilize workers around concrete issues like urban redevelopment and health care, thereby

---

[363] Heather Booth, autobiographical article, Veteran Feminists of America, www.vfa.us/ICONS.htm

[364] Natalie Doss, "The Progressive: For over forty years, Heather Booth has worked to build a small-d democracy," *Chicago Weekly*, 1-7-10

[365] Heather Booth, Paul Booth, Harry Boyte, Sara Boyte, Steve Max, and Roger Robinson, *Socialism and the Coming Decade,* 1969. Heather Booth also wrote a book with Boyte and Max, *Citizen Action and the New American Populism*, Temple University Press, 1986.

giving "the socialist movement relevance to the daily lives of the people." Over time, patient neighborhood organizing and struggle will prepare the workers' consciousness for the socialist revolution to come. [366]

To realize that "organization of socialists" and to spread Gramscian Marxism, Paul Booth and Harry Boyte helped establish the New American Movement (NAM) in 1971. [367] Boyte co-authored NAM's first mission statement, arguing that the transition to socialism demanded more than simply organizing the industrial workforce but required organizing "new forms of culture and community." [368]

"New forms of culture" took many shapes. For instance, Heather was a founding member of NAM's "loosely connected" feminist-education program, the Chicago Women's Liberation Union, and her abortion counseling service "Jane" became one of its projects, itself providing underground illegal abortions. [369]

Within a decade, NAM merged with Michael Harrington's Democratic Socialist Organizing Committee (DSOC), forming the current Democratic Socialists of America (DSA), the largest

---

[366] Stanley Kurtz, *Radical-in-Chief: Barack Obama and the Untold Story of American Socialism*, Threshold Editions – Division of Simon and Schuster, 2010, p 137.

[367] Victor Cohen, "The New American Movement and the Los Angeles Socialist Community School," *Minnesota Review*, Fall/Winter 2007, www.theminnesotareview.org/journal/ns69/cohen.shtml#; *Radical-in-Chief*...p. 143.

[368] The New American Movement..."

[369] CWLU Herstory Project, Introduction: www.cwluherstory.org/Historical-Context; "The New American Movement..."

socialist party in the United States.[370] The Booths continued to support the DSA and spoke at its various functions[371] and Steve Max became a DSA Vice-Chair.[372]

Saul Alinsky came into the Booths' lives early in their careers through the person of Margery Tabankin, an IAF organizer.[373] Tabankin worked with Alinsky on a 1970 Chicago Campaign Against Pollution, renamed Citizens Action Program (CAP). The IAF provided CAP with staff and Paul Booth became the organization's first co-chair.[374] The following year, the same year that Alinsky published *Rules for Radicals*, Heather Booth trained at his Chicago-based, organizer-training institute. [375] She found his organizational theories to be a revelation, remarking, "Alinsky is to community organizing as Freud is to psychoanalysis."[376]

---

[370] Victor Cohen, "The New American Movement and the Los Angeles Socialist Community School," *Minnesota Review*, Fall/Winter 2007, www.theminnesotareview.org/journal/ns69/cohen.shtml#

[371] November 16-18, 1979 DSA conference in Washington, DC included a workshop that had Heather Booth as one of its speakers. The Chicago DSA 29th Annual Norman Thomas - Eugene V. Debs Dinner in 1987 had Heather Booth as an honoree. Paul Booth was confirmed as a DSA member in 1990 [8th Socialist Scholars Conference, April 6-8, 1990, conference program] and the Chicago DSA's publication *New Ground,* Spring 1992 includes the article "Heather Booth, Jackie Grimshaw and Michael Dyson Wow Crowd at the University of Chicago." The event referred to was sponsored by the University of Chicago DSA.

[372] www.dsa.org; The first plenary session of the 2010 Young Democrat Socialists of America Conference was opened with Steve Max.

[373] Gary Delgado, *Organizing the Movement: The Roots and Growth of ACORN,* (Temple University Press: 1986), pp 22-23.

[374] Harry C. Boyte, *The Backyard Revolution: Understanding the New Citizen* Movement (Philadelphia: Temple University, 1980), p. 57-58; *Organizing the Movement*...p 23.

[375] Stanford D. Horwitt, *Let Them Call Me Rebel*, (Vintage Books: 1989), p 545.

[376] *Backyard Revolution*..., p 39.

Heather and Steve Max founded the Midwest Academy in 1973. Max was the Academy's first trainer, later the director of its Political Education Project,[377] and is its current Associate Director.

> Steve Max, the main Academy teacher, who himself helped found the Students for a Democratic Society, adds a wealth of practical detail from years of experience in election campaigns, union battles, and community fights.[378]

For her part, Booth developed a curriculum to train organizers "with a political and economic context, and teach the skills necessary for effective organizing." Midwest Academy – which trained many leaders of the women's movement in addition to Alinskyian community organizers[379] – also sought to build "a network across many different kinds of organizations in which activists could share their experiences, develop relationships, and shape a vision not bound by the limitations of any one form of organizing."[380]

Meanwhile, Paul Booth was involved in the labor movement, acting as Research Director for the United Packinghouse

---

[377] Interviewee biographies from *Rebels with a Cause*, a documentary narrated by members of Students for a Democratic Society (SDS), produced, directed, and edited by Helen Garvy (2000).

[378] *Backyard Revolution…*, p 110.

[379] Stephanie Gilmore, Sara Evans, *Feminist coalitions: historical perspectives on second-wave feminism in United States*, University of Illinois Press, 2008. Gilmore writes: "By 1975, the Midwest Academy appeared to be focused on the women's movement and labor organizing.

[380] "About Us," Midwest Academy, www.midwestacademy.com/about-us (accessed 3-16-11).

Workers of America in the late 60s and then joining the American Federation of State, County and Municipal Employees (AFSCME) in 1974, where he served as organizing director for 10 years and is currently an assistant to the union's president. [381]

Margery Tabankin had also been a member of the SDS, joining the radical student organization while studying at the University of Wisconsin and then:

> In late 1969, she was picked to become one of the first women student trainees at master leftist activist Saul Alinsky's School of Community Organizing in Chicago, where she learned how to form grass-roots efforts and drum up community support. [382]

The internship was cut short because of family issues but by 1972 she had become director of the Youth Project, which funded a variety of progressive organizations, [383] among them Midwest Academy, [384] ACORN [385] and ACORN's Institute for

---

[381] Midwest Academy Board of Directors' Bios, www.midwestacademy.com/board-directors; Jim McNeill, "Labor Divided," *Dissent Magazine*, Fall 2005.

[382] Nikki Finke, "A Radical Move: Margery Tabankin Has Fled the Center of Power for the Center of Status, but Without Missing an Activist Beat," *LA Times,* 8-13-89.

[383] "A Radical Move…;" Laurene Conner, "Building the New American Experiment," *The Wanderer,* 9-9-89. The Youth Project received over half a million (Catholic) Campaign for Human Development dollars between 1982-1985.

[384] William T. Poole and Thomas W. Pauken, *The Campaign for Human Development: Christian Charity or Political Activism,* Studies in Organization Trends #4, Capital Research Center, 1988, p. 25, citing the Annual Report of the Youth Project, 1974, p. 50 (no amount specified); 1975, pp 25-26 (no amount specified); 1977, p 28 (no amount specified); 1979, p 81 & 83 (no amount specified); 1980/1981, p 47 (CR Fund $10,000), p. 52 (Resource Fund $10,000), and p. 57 (Sunrise Fund $10,000); 1985/1986, p. 30

Social Justice,[386] and a front group for the Trotskyite Communist Socialist Workers Party, the Political Rights Defense Fund[387] - among numerous others. The Youth Project, in other words, "was a funnel for tax-exempt money to go to radical groups, many of them not tax-exempt," including community organizing groups.[388]

Tabankin moved on to the directorship of Americorps VISTA (Volunteer in Service to America), from 1977 -1981,[389] and

---

(LMLSP Fund $1,000); 1986/1987, p. 25 (Donor Advised Funds, Citizen Participation Category $8,500).

[385] *Campaign for Human Development: Christian Charity or Political Activism...*, citing the Annual Report of the Youth Project, 1974, p. 6-7 (no amount specified); 1975, pp 1-2 (no amount specified); 1976, p 16 (no amount specified); 1977, p 20, 25 (no amount specified); 1978, p 13 (no amount specified) and p. 61 (Tax Reform Program, no amount specified); 1979, p 14-15 (no amount specified) and p. 76 (Tax Reform Program, no amount specified); 1981/1982, p 16 (Western Office $3,000); 1983/1984, p. 19 (Southern Office $10,000).

[386] *Campaign for Human Development: Christian Charity or Political Activism...*, citing the Annual Report of the Youth Project, 1976, p. 38 (South West Fund, no amount specified); 1977, pp 49 (South West Fund, no amount specified); 1978, p 66 (CR Fund, two commitments, no amounts specified); 1980/1981, p 46 (CR Fund, $15,000), p. 56 (Sunrise Fund $10,000), and p. 57 (Sunrise Fund $4,000); 1981/1982, p 27 (Eastern Office $4,000) and p. 48 (Scally Fund $2,500); 1982/1983, p. 42 (Eleven Twenty-Two Fund $5,000); 1983/1984, p. 23 (Eastern Office $2,000) and p. 36 (Pearl River Fund $10,000); 1984/1985 p. 22 (Southern Region $3,000) and p. 31 (Pearl River Fund $11,000);1985/1986 p. 27 (Circle Fund, $10,000), p. 29 (Fieldwood Fund ($10,000), and p. 31 ((Pearl River Fund $12,000).

[387] *The Campaign for Human Development: Christian Charity or Political Activism...* p. 25, citing Richard F. Staar, Ed., Yearbook on International Communist Affairs, 1979 (Stanford, California: Hoover Institution Press, 1979).

[388] Rael Jean and Erich Isaac, *The Coercive Utopians: Social Deception by America's Power Players*, (Discipleship Books (An Imprint of Regnery): 1985), p187

[389] "A Radical Move..."

under her tenure, the Midwest Academy received $600,000 to train VISTA volunteers.[390]

CITIZEN ACTION

The roots of Citizen Action lie in the 1978 Midwest Academy's Citizen/Labor Energy Coalition (C/LEC), which had Heather Booth as its first director until 1981[391] and received critical funding and networking from The Youth Project.[392] C/LEC brought local neighborhood groups and organized labor into a national organization that had the support of the UAW (International Union, United Automobile, Aerospace and Agricultural Implement Workers of America) and Paul Booth's public service union.[393]

C/LEC's goal was "to build a movement that will manifest itself in a noticeable shift in public opinion and emergence of national leaders with 'progressive tendencies."[394]

> The Midwest Academy joined with labor unions and national public interest, consumer, and environmental groups in the fall of 1977 to begin work on a national energy coalition that could fight for democratic alternatives to policies

---

[390] *The Coercive Utopians...*

[391] *The Campaign for Human Development: Christian Charity or Political Activism*...p. 32-33. Referencing material in Boyte, Booth, and Max, *Citizen Action and the New American Populism,* (Philadelphia: Temple University Press, 1986), p. 107.

[392] *The Campaign for Human Development: Christian Charity or* ....p. 31; quoting from the 1979 *Youth Project Annual Report,* p 22.

[393] *Organizing the Movement*...p. 216.

[394] "Building the New American Experiment..."

advocated by the energy giants.[395]

One year later, the five initial C/LEC state groups – Oregon Fair Share, Massachusetts Fair Share, Illinois Public Action Council, Connecticut Citizen Action Coalition, and Ohio Public Interest Campaign – formed Citizen Action:.[396]

> "Citizen Action is seen as an organizing committee," explained Heather Booth, founder of the Midwest Academy, which was involved in its formation. "Partly it is intended to help new state groups get going elsewhere."[397]

One Citizen Action trainer, Jackie Kendall – who was Executive Director of the Midwest Academy from 1982-2010[398] – was more explicit. The goal of Citizen Action was "to build a long-term, direct action organization that can change the system of power."[399]

Heather Booth was one of Citizen Action's founders, a co-director, its president from 1979-1988 and, together with Paul Booth and Steve Max, was a leading activist for the

---

[395] *The Backyard Revolution...*, p. 103

[396] Ron Arnold, *Undue Influence: Wealthy Foundations, Grant Driven Environmental Groups, and Zealous Bureaucrats That Control Your Future*, (Free Enterprise Press: 1999).

[397] *Backyard Revolution...*p101

[398] Midwest Academy Board of Directors' Bios...

[399] "Troublemakers in Training...," p. 40.

organization.[400] Booth's Midwest Academy was Citizen Action's "training arm."[401]

In 1997, Citizen Action was hit with scandal over a campaign money-laundering scheme and closed its national office in Washington.

> [T]he group was involved in a scheme to help fund the 1996 reelection campaign of Teamsters president Ron Carey. Carey has resigned, three of his aides have pleaded guilty to conspiracy and other charges, and a federal investigation into the scandal continues even as some former affiliates of Citizen Action attempt to come to grips with what went wrong with the grassroots group and why.

> "Before the Teamsters scandal, there were problems" at Citizen Action, said Edward Kelly, former director of the Massachusetts chapter. "Basically, I saw national go from a nonpartisan, grass-roots organization to a partisan one tied to the Democratic Party. I didn't like that."

> .... According to the Teamsters federal investigation, Citizen Action received $475,000 from the International Brotherhood of Teamsters last year in support of the consumer group's Campaign for a Responsible Congress, which was developed to help

---

[400] Jean-Christophe Agnew, Roy Rosenzweig, "A companion to post-1945 America," (Blackwell Publishing: 2002), p 291.

[401] Bernard Ohanian, "Troublemakers in Training," *Mother Jones,* January 1988, p. 40.

defeat the elections of GOP candidates to the House of Representatives. [402]

There were other problems, as well. "[U]nder the normal guise of nonpartisanship, national [Citizen Action] was only tracking what the Democratic Party was saying about the Republicans. It was determined to help defeat incumbent Republicans, but the material Citizen Action was putting out was almost indistinguishable from the information we were seeing from the DNC," one former state affiliate director complained. Another director resigned after a federal probe of an alleged $2.7 million check kiting scheme. [103]

USACTION

Undaunted, Heather Booth revived Citizen Action in 1999 under the name USAction, and serves as a vice president. [404] This round, USAction created a labyrinth of related organizations and projects. From its inception, USAction has been the 501(c)(4) political entity; its 501(c)(3)sister organization, the USAction Education Fund, was designed to handle "research and technical assistance."[405]

In 2007, USAction and USAction Education Fund (USAEF)[406] developed a joint, 501c-4 project called

---

[402] Diane E. Lewis, "Scandal Unravels Liberal Consumer Group," *Boston Globe,* 12-6-97.
[403] "Scandal Unravels..."
[404] As of 2011, Booth continues in this capacity.
[405] "Bad Policy, Bad Medicine: Bush Plans for Taxes and Prescription Drugs Unfair to Working Families
and Seniors," USAction Report in Conjunction with Citizens A for Tax Justice, February 2001
[406] www.truemajority.org (accessed 6-1-11)

TrueMajority,[407] for the purpose of "organiz[ing] activists online to support Investment in America's Future."[408]

All three organizations have the same Washington DC address, phone number, and state-based affiliates and partners – among them the Midwest Academy.[409] In some situations, they refer to themselves as USAction/TrueMajority.[410]

The projects of USAction are varied and ambitious. It founded the coalition Health Care for America Now (HCAN) in 2008 to generate public support for what was to become the Affordable Health Care for America Act[411] of 2009. Jeff Blum, executive director of USAction[412] and USAction Education Fund,[413] acted as HCAN's steering committee co-chair.[414]

HCAN was a coalition "of unions, think tanks and other groups"[415] that included the Planned Parenthood of America Federation and the Alinskyian organizing networks of ACORN, USAction (obviously), the Center for Community Change –

---

[407] www.truemajority.org/who

[408] www.usaction.org/site/pp.asp.103.html The website of TrueMajority is www.truemajorityaction.org and www.truemajority.org. Both go to the same page.

[409] Affiliate and partner list for USAction: www.usaction.org/site/pp.asp.112.html; affiliate and partner list for USAction Education Fund: www.usactioneducationfund.org/site/pp.asp.135.html

[410] act.truemajorityaction.org/p/dia/action3/common/public/ ?action_KEY=159

[411] HR 3962

[412] Neil Payne, "Want to Cut Federal Spending? Go Where the Money Is," USAction blog, 4-28-11: insideusaction.org/aggprog/?p=183

[413] USAction Education Fund Press Release, "USAEF's Blum Says Massive Voter Turnout 'No Accident'," 11/3/2004.

[414] David Elliot, "Sen. Edward Kennedy - May His Dreams & His Work Live On," Aggressive Progressive, blog of TrueMajority, 8-26-09, www.truemajority.org/aggressiveprogressive/?p=308; USAction Issue Campaigns: www.usaction.org/site/pp.asp.133.html.

[415] Reuters, "Coalition to lobby for U.S. health-care reform," 7-8-08.

itself a coalition that includes a number of the Alinskyian organizing networks, specifically ACORN, the Gamaliel Foundation and various Gamaliel affiliates – Northwest Federation of Community Organizations, and Jobs for Justice, along with local affiliates of these groups.[416]

Publicity about coalition efforts to pass health care legislation claimed it would spend $40 million on a one-year multimedia campaign. Steering committee members – ACORN, AFSCME, Americans United for Change, Campaign for America's Future, Center for American Progress Action Fund, MoveOn.org, National Council of La Raza, National Education Association, Planned Parenthood Federation of America, Service Employees International Union, United Food and Commercial Workers, and USAction – committed at least $500,000 each.[417] Philanthropic foundations made up the rest.[418]

At the conclusion of this campaign, one funder commissioned an evaluation of the HCAN's efforts and found that it "made a difference…. mobilizing the progressive base, assembling a progressive coalition, and keeping it united and engaged." The coalition "helped establish health care as a legislative priority, frame the debate, and build momentum for reform efforts" during the 2008 elections and in the subsequent Congressional session.[419]

---

[416] Health Care for America Now website, "Who We Are" listing of coalition members: healthcareforamericanow.org/site/content/who_we_are

[417] Progressive Maryland Press Release, "$40 Million Health Care Campaign Launched in Maryland and Nationwide," 7-8-08.

[418] Atlantic Philanthropies provided $10 million. According to HCAN's tax disclaimer, "HCAN is related to Health Care for America Education Fund, a project of The Tides Center, a section 501(c)(3) public charity." (healthcareforamericanow.org/site/content/more_about_hcan)

[419] "HCAN Evaluation: Executive Summary - An overview of the comprehensive qualitative evaluation of the Health Care for America Now

HCAN's partnering with the national Alinskyian organizing networks of ACORN, the Center for Community Change (CCC), Northwest Federation of Community Organizations (NWFCO), and USAction was part of the overall strategy. "Investing in national networks with state-based organizations allowed HCAN to maximize the benefits of local knowledge and pre-existing infrastructure in the states."[420]

Jobs for America Now is another coalition comprised of the same Alinskyian cast of characters – the Center for Community Change with its ACORN, Gamaliel Foundation and various Gamaliel affiliates members, Interfaith Worker Justice, and USAction – as well as heavy union representation.[421] Alan Charney, USAction's program director, has been Jobs for America Now's interim campaign manager.[422]

Like HCAN, Jobs for America Now is also concerned about passing legislation, such as the proposed and failed 2010 Local Jobs for America Act[423] that critics called "a gigantic bailout of government employees and union jobs."[424]

USAction is a partner of Americans for Responsible Taxes – along with the other groups that seem to be found so frequently working together, including the big unions (AFL-CIO, SEIU, Paul Booth's AFSCME, among others), George Soros' Center for American Progress, and Sojourners.   Americans for

---

campaign," Prepared for The Atlantic Philanthropies by Grassroots Solution and M+R Strategic Services, 2010.

[420] "HCAN Evaluation: Executive Summary…"

[421] www.jobs4americanow.org/organizations

[422] USAction Press release, "Groups Announce Broad New Coalition, National Push for Jobs Legislation," 12-16-09

[423] H.R. 4812. Isaiah J. Poole, "This Jobs Bill Could Work," Campaign for America's Future blog, 3-10-10.

[424] Don't Tread on Me, Blog of the New Hampshire Tea Party, "New Bailout: the Local Jobs for America Act," 5-6-10.

Responsible Taxes is particularly concerned with repealing "Bush tax cuts for the rich."[425]

USAction Education Fund endorses One Nation, a coalition that says it "seeks to transcend superficial differences and bring us together in a common quest for equal opportunity and justice for all."[426] The superficial differences to be transcended involve "competing agendas" within the progressive movement. One Nation wants to help that movement "find its voice again" and "counter the Tea Party narrative."[427] Again, coalition members include various unions, the Center for Community Change, and Sojourners.[428]

Perhaps most striking of all is the Community Action Partnership, a network of regional and state "community action agencies"[429] together with a number of nonprofits – including USAction and George Soros' Center for American Progress – and several federal government departments such as Health and Human Services, Housing and Urban Development, and the US Department of Treasury.[430] The community action agencies

---

[425] The phrase "Bush tax cuts for the rich" is repeated again and again in Americans for Responsible Taxes literature. One example from the ART website, "Update: August 30, 2010, Podesta/Greenstein "Bush Tax Cuts for the Rich Must Go:" www.responsibletaxes.org/resources/august-30-update

[426] www.usactioneducationfund.org

[427] Krissah Thompson, "Progressives hope 'One Nation' coalition can recapture grass-roots fervor,"
Washington Post, 7-12-10.

[428] action.onenationworkingtogether.org/organizations

[429] These community action agencies were established under the Economic Opportunity Act of 1964 to fight America's War on Poverty:
www.communityactionpartnership.com/index.php?option=com_content&task=view&id=21&Itemid=50

[430] www.communityactionpartnership.com/
index.php?option=com_content&task=view&id=67&Itemid=174;

provide a variety of services to address the needs of poor communities, such as emergency services, food access, job training, and housing assistance. Ninety-four percent of these community action agencies are engaged in some form of "community coordination," namely "citizen participation," and "neighborhood and community organization."[431]

The above, brief history doesn't begin to convey the breadth of the Booth's – and of the Midwest Academy's – influence. Midwest Academy helped to build both the field operations and the strategic plans for such organizations as Sierra Club, NARAL, and the United States Student Organization. [432] In 1986, Midwest Academy cosponsored Grassroots Organizing Weekends (GROW) to train campus leaders.[433] In 1990 Heather Booth was Director of the Coalition for Democratic Values, a partisan organization of leading far-left Democrats and from 1993, during the Clinton administration, she worked on electoral campaigns and with the Democratic National Committee as its training director and grass-roots specialist.[434]

Heather served on the National Housing Institute Board.[435] During the 90s, the US Department of Housing and Urban Development (HUD) listed Sue Maxwell, a Midwest Academy

---

www.communityactionpartnership.com/index.php?option=com_content&task=view&id=23&Itemid=175

[431] www.communityactionpartnership.com/index.php?option=com_content&task=view&id=21&Itemid=50

[432] "Heather Booth, on canvassing & canvassers," *Canvassing Works,* 3-19-07: www.canvassingworks.org/canvassingworks/2007/03/for_40_years_he.html

[433] Angus Johnston, "A Brief History of NSA [National Student Association] and USSA [US Student Association]," essential.org/org/history.htm.

[434] "Delegates see political problems, promise of '96," *AFL-CIO News,* 3-29-96

[435] The National Housing Institute, "About NHI," www.nhi.org/about/nhi.html (accessed 1997)

trainer, as the contact for the HUD Training Academy.[436] Around the same time, Kim Bobo – then of the Midwest Academy – assisted in publishing the manual, *How to Win: A Practical Guide for Defeating the Radical Right in Your Community*. The guide defined "radical right" as any group that had, among other things, a pro-life or morally traditional perspective.[437] In 2000, Heather Booth was founding director of the NAACP National Voter Fund.[438] She was Field Director for Sen. Carol Moseley Braun's successful Senate race. She has been a consultant to Center for Community Change, advising on the development of the Community Voting Project as well as serving on its Board,[439] and an adviser to many other groups, including MoveOn.org, the Campaign for Comprehensive Immigration Reform, Campaign for America's Future, and NOW.[440] We are only skimming the surface.

As is apparent from even this cursory account, there's been a good bit of cross-fertilization between Heather Booth's training of community organizers and Paul Booth's union work. From the very beginning of their relationship in 1966, the two presented a workshop for the AFL-CIO together, discussing strategies for mobilizing workers and allies around labor

---

[436] US Department of Housing and Urban Development, www.hud.gov/directory/dirmwest.html, accessed 3-8-97.
[437] Matthew Freeman, "How to Win: A Practical Guide for Defeating the Radical Right in Your Community, Ten Things to do When the Right Comes to Town,*"People For the American Way,* 1994.
[438] Heather Booth, Statement, Jewish Women Archive: Jewish Women and the Feminist Revolution, undated.
[439] Center for Community Change: www.communitychange.org/who-we-are/our-board
[440] From Midwest Academy Board of Director biographies: www.midwestacademy.com/board-directors

issues.[441]   More than 40 years later, Heather Booth acted as director of the AFL-CIO's Health Care Reform Campaign.[442] She is also the founding director of Americans for Financial Reform, a coalition "fighting to regulate the financial industry"[443] that includes the AFL-CIO, her husband's AFSCME and her own USAction.[444]   Citizen Action/USAction, therefore, blends community organizing with labor organizing to create a potent political force in the progressive partisan political movement.

Chronology of Heather and Paul Booth		
	Heather	**Paul**
1960s	Heather assists women in procuring illegal abortions ("Jane")	
1966	Heather meets SDS activist Paul Booth at University of Chicago	
1969	Heather Booth, Paul Booth, Harry Boyte, Sara Boyte, Steve Max, and Roger Robinson coauthor *Socialism and the Coming Decade*.	
1970		Paul and IAF organizer Margery Tabankin work with Alinsky on the Chicago Campaign Against Pollution, renamed Citizens Action Program (CAP).

---

[441] "Delegates see political problems, promise of '96," *AFL-CIO News*, 3-29-96.
[442] AFL-CIO News Release, "AFL-CIO Declares '08 Elections a Mandate for High Quality Health Care for All by '09," 8-30-07.
[443] Heather Booth bio, New Organizing Institute Staff: www.neworganizing.com/profile/Heather-Booth
[444] Americans for Financial Security, coalition members: ourfinancialsecurity.org

1971	Heather, Paul Booth, and Harry Boyte are founding members of the New American Movement (which merges in the 80s with Michael Harrington's Democratic Socialist Organizing Committee (DSOC) to form the Democratic Socialists of America (DSA).	
1973	Heather Booth and former SDS field secretary Steve Max found the Midwest Academy. Max was the Academy's first trainer, director of its Political Education Project, and is its current Associate Director.	
1974		Paul Booth was Research Director for the United Packinghouse Workers of America in the late 60s and then joined the American Federation of State, County and Municipal Employees (AFSCME) in 1974, where he served as organizing director for 10 years and is currently assistant to the union's president.
1978	Midwest Academy founds Citizen/Labor Energy Coalition (C/LEC), a national coalition of neighborhood groups and organized labor which had Heather Booth as its first director until 1981	

1979	Several C/LEC locals form Citizen Action. Heather Booth, a Citizen Action cofounder, serves as CA president from 1979-1988	Paul Booth and Steve Max were Citizen Action activists and the Midwest Academy its "training arm"
1991	Kim Bobo, trainer for the Midwest Academy, founds the Chicago Interfaith Committee on Worker Issues	
1996	The Chicago Interfaith Committee on Worker Issues expands to become the National Interfaith Committee for Worker Justice (later renamed Interfaith Worker Justice - IWJ)	
1997	Citizen Action is embroiled in scandal	
1993	Heather Booth has worked on electoral campaigns for the Democratic National Committee and has served as its grass-roots specialist. Northwest Federation of Community Organizations is founded.	
1999	Heather Booth revives Citizen Action under the name USAction, and serves as a vice president	
2010	Heather Booth became founding director for the Americans for Financial Reform coalition	
2010	Northwest Federation of Community Organizations expands and becomes Alliance for a Just Society	

INTERFAITH WORKER JUSTICE

As explained above, the Midwest Academy spawned and influenced a remarkable number of organizations and, thanks to the marriage of Heather and Paul Booth, has nurtured a strong relationship between community organizing and union work. The Interfaith Worker Justice (IWJ, called the National Interfaith Committee for Worker Justice until 1995) is one of the more significant of these, drawing together many of the Booths' foci. Developed from the Chicago Interfaith Committee on Worker Issues in 1991,[445] its founder[446] and executive director, Kim Bobo, was a Midwest Academy trainer.[447]

The idea behind the National Interfaith Committee for Worker Justice/IWJ was "to facilitate relationships between local religious leaders and labor unions throughout the United States."[448]

An example of this "relationship" may be found in a class launched jointly by the Association of Chicago Theological Schools (ACTS) and IWJ. ACTS is a cooperative effort among

---

[445] "Interfaith Worker Justice: Organizational Profile," Marguerite Casey Foundation, 2005. The local Chicago Interfaith Committee on Worker Issues was itself renamed to ARISE Chicago: arisechicago.org/worker-center (accessed 9-6-11)

[446] Chicago Interfaith Committee on Worker Issues, today called Arise Chicago, continues as a separate but affiliated organization. It was founded by Monsignor Jack Egan, Rabbi Robert Marx, United Methodist Bishop Jesse DeWitt and **Kim Bobo**: arisechicago.org.

[447] Interfaith Worker Justice, "For You Were Once a Stranger: Immigration in the US through the Lens of Faith," 2007, author bios, p. 111.

[448] George E. Schultze, SJ, "Work, Worship, and *Laborem Exercens* in the United States Today," working draft paper, University of San Francisco, undated.

Catholic, Evangelical, Lutheran, Baptist, United Church of
Christ, Episcopalian, and Unitarian member institutions[449] and
all these religious bodies have generously contributed to IWJ's
work.[450] The ACTS/IWJ class explores "the pastoral and
prophetic, the theological and the ethical issues clergy will face
when interacting with the work life of congregants and
neighbors." [451]

Over the years, these "relationships" have made for some
interesting – if disturbing – couplings. "Unions are
...cultivating the next generation of church leaders," writes one
observer, pointing to IWJ's "Seminary Summer," an
arrangement by which seminarians spend their summer with
union locals.

> "Within three years most of these students will
> be in leadership positions in congregations,"
> predicted IWJ head Kim Bobo shortly after the
> program began in 2000. Since then, some 200
> seminarians have helped unionize Mississippi
> poultry workers, aided the Service Employees
> International Union in organizing Georgia
> public-sector employees, and bolstered
> campaigns for living-wage legislation in
> California municipalities. [452]

The strategy of engaging the religious left has been so
successful that IWJ and its labor colleagues founded over 60
local affiliates – like the other Alinskyian organizing networks,

---

[449] Association of Chicago Theological Schools: www.actschicago.org
[450] Annual reports are regularly published in the IWJ newsletter, *FaithWorks*,
and show grant from each of these entities.
[451] Interfaith Workers Justice newsletter, *FaithWorks*, March 2005.
[452] Steven Malanga, "The Religious Left, Reborn," *City Journal*, Autumn,
2007.

IWJ has scores of locals all over the country.[453]

> The Wayne State University Labor Studies
> Center's "activist handbook" advises living-wage
> campaigns always to put religious leaders out
> front. "As soon as you have clergy arguing for
> something called a 'living wage,' you've lost the
> battle if you're representing businesses."[454]

It's all about strategy, not religious values, *per se*:

> "When you have a faith community, it adds a
> moral and ethical component"—all the more
> effective in that the Religious Left essentially
> has the spiritual terrain to itself on economic
> matters, which Christian conservative groups
> have mostly ignored. …Having established
> itself in many places as the moral authority on
> economic issues, the resurgent Religious Left
> has brought back the fiery redistributionist
> language of the social gospel. [455]

To assure that the religious voice was used to its own
purposes, the National Interfaith Committee for Worker Justice
(IWJ) founding Board of Directors included Monsignor Jack

---

[453] IWJ website, "History," www.iwj.org/template/page.cfm?id=93: "In just eleven years, IWJ has organized a national network of more than 70 interfaith committees, workers' centers and student groups, making it the leading national organization working to strengthen the religious community's involvement in issues of workplace justice…"

[454] "The Religious Left, Reborn…"

[455] "The Religious Left, Reborn…"

Egan – one of Saul Alinsky's staunchest disciples and a premier force behind the Catholic Church's dissenting Call to Action movement. "Labor priest" Monsignor George Higgins was another and Monsignor Phil Murnion, who was director of the National Pastoral Life Center and another Call to Action supporter, were others.[456] It's no coincidence that Kim Bobo, National Interfaith Committee for Worker Justice founder and executive director,[457] for years has also been listed as a speaker for Call to Action's referral service.[458]

The efforts of National Interfaith Committee for Worker Justice/Interfaith Worker Justice have consistently been directed toward progressive political solutions. In 1991, while working for Midwest Academy, Bobo coauthored *Organizing for Social Change: A Manual for Activists in the 1990's.*[459] A few years later, Bobo is acknowledged for her "inspiration" in preparing the – among other things, pro-abortion – activist handbook *How to Win: A Practical Guide for Defeating the Radical Right in Your Community*. Her particular contribution concerned the involvement of religious communities. [460]

Bobo has challenged what she calls "conservative Christian forces" that are "monopolizing the morality-in-politics debate around such issues as abortion rights and same-sex marriage," believing instead that Christians ought to focus more on

---

[456] IWJ website, "History," www.iwj.org/template/page.cfm?id=93

[457] Bobo continues as the executive director of IWJ as of 2011.

[458] Call to Action, Speakers and Artists Referral Service: www.cta-usa.org/resstars.html (accessed 10-4-11).

[459] Kim Bobo, Jackie Kendall, Steve Max, *Organizing for Social Change: A Manual for Activists in the 1990's,* Seven Locks Press, 1991 (copyright held by the Midwest Academy). Chapter 17 is "Working with Religious Organizations."

[460] Radical Right Task Force, *How to Win: A Practical Guide for Defeating the Radical Right in Your Community*, 1994.

economic justice.[461]

It is against this background that the work of Interfaith Worker Justice (IWJ) is understood. IWJ was a major proponent for the proposed legislation, Employee Free Choice Act, claiming that the bill "would restore the ability of workers to form unions without the threats, harassment and intimidation that too many employers now routinely use to sabotage union organizing." IWJ formed a religious leaders "spokesperson team" to convey its message.[462]

The IWJ website prepared a number of printed resources targeted at "conservative Christian" congregations. There was a set of "questions and answers that clarify the importance of the Employee Free Choice Act for working people" and another version "formatted as a bulletin insert." There was also "a step-by-step guide [to]…explain how to organize a delegation of religious leaders and congregational members to engage [its]…senators" about the proposed legislation. Lastly, there were supportive statements from numerous "faith leaders" – presumably useful for demonstrating how compatible the legislation was with various faith traditions – no matter how "conservative" they may be.[463]

IWJ also has resources to address the broader economic situation of the United States. A collection of materials called the Unemployment and the Economic Crisis: a Congregational

---

[461] Don Lattin, "Pushing poverty into 'moral-values' debate: Some religious leaders trying to broaden discussion beyond abortion and marriage," San Francisco Chronicle, 12-12-04.

[462] IWJ information about the Employee Free Choice Act, posted at Latin Webzine: http://directory.lwchicago.com/Interfaith-Worker-Justice-1785.html

[463] Interfaith Worker Justice website, Employee Free Choice Act, links to supportive materials: http://www.iwj.org/template/page.cfm?id=203 (accessed 10-10-11)

Toolkit provides a guide to one's legal rights following job loss – including information about unemployment compensation, foreclosure, and health insurance – another guide for congregational support groups, an exhortation to activism, and some prayers. There's also a "reflection piece."[464]

Some of this material is, obviously, useful. It's laudable for a congregation to have concrete advice and assistance for newly unemployed workers and their families.

What is problematic is the IWJ's use of these materials to advance their own agenda as if it were on a level with "Church teaching." The "reflective piece," "The Spiritual Meaning of the Economic Crisis," is worth quoting in some detail:

> The Book of Exodus and the Holy Qu'ran both tell the story of how the people of God, liberated from bondage in Egypt, lost their way and turned to the worship of idols as they awaited the return of Moses from the holy mountain. They fashioned a Golden Calf.
>
> Like the Israelites in the desert, we have lost our way and fallen into idolatry. **The golden calf that is worshipped in the United States** and across much of the world **is now known as "the free market."** The cry went out, "Unfetter our businesses and entrepreneurs, cut taxes for the wealthy, and all will share in the prosperity of our 'opportunity society.'" Hedge fund managers and investment bankers went giddy over their huge windfalls, building a house of cards that has now come tumbling down. **We**

---

[464] IWJ, *Unemployment and the Economic Crisis: a Congregational Toolkit:* http://www.iwj.org/template/page.cfm?id=201

worship wealth, and have lost sight of the fact that we are all children of God, and that we are all in this together. [emphasis added][465]

This classic liberationist "reflection" performs a very untraditional scripture exegesis: "The golden calf that is worshipped in the United States… is now known as 'the free market.'" "We worship wealth…" The IWJ material leaves worshippers with the impression that their faith teaches them that preference for, or support of, a "free market system" is idolatrous, materialistic, sinful, and this is the reason we are being punished by God with economic collapse.

Then the IWJ material redefines righteousness:

> As people of faith, we call on our public leaders to lift up the workers and the poor. It is not enough to say jobs must be created. The Israelites in Egypt worked every day in a full employment economy known as slavery.
>
> The economic program we need must create living wage jobs that allow workers to support themselves and their families in dignity, not in poverty. Unions are not the problem, and they must be part of the solution. Workers create wealth and must be allowed a fair share of what they create.[466]

Specifically, "to help heal this economy and repair the torn

---

[465] IWJ, "The Spiritual Meaning of the Economic Crisis," undated, p. 2: www.iwj.org/template/guard_process2.cfm?where=inline

[466] "The Spiritual Meaning of the Economic Crisis…," p. 2.

fabric of our society"[467] religious people must pass the *Employee Free Choice Act*, pass a jobs creation package, institute universal health care, and so forth.

> We call on all people of faith and good will to stand with us and proclaim, with the prophet Amos and Dr. Martin Luther King, Jr.: Let justice roll down like waters, and righteousness like a mighty stream. (Amos 5:24).[468]

The Employee Free Choice Act is not, however, a litmus test of religiously-informed ethics or even of purely secular concern for one's fellow citizens. People of good will may righteously believe the legislation to be harmful, contending that rather than support workers' freedom to decide whether to bargain collectively with their employers, the Employee Free Choice Act would permit unions to organize by means of publically signed "card-check campaigns" that leave workers vulnerable to union pressure while a secret ballot safeguards against intimidation.[469]

Further, a critic might argue that the Employee Free Choice Act also mandates binding arbitration after 90 days of unresolved negotiation, without the option of any appeal. Such a move, ironically, strips workers of any real right to bargain collectively by compelling them to accept government-imposed terms. Why would the union machines (as opposed to their membership) and the IWJ support such a thing?

---

[467] "The Spiritual Meaning of the Economic Crisis…," p.3.

[468] "The Spiritual Meaning of the Economic Crisis…," p. 4.

[469] One negative analysis of the Employee Free Choice Act was prepared by James Sherk *and* Paul Kersey, "How the Employee Free Choice Act Takes Away Workers' Rights," Heritage Foundation, 4-23-07:
http://www.heritage.org/research/reports/2007/04/full-text-how-the-employee-free-choice-act-takes-away-workers-rights

These are legitimate concerns that give rise to opposing viewpoints. The work of civic engagement is to debate these viewpoints in search of greater good. Instead, religious concepts are used manipulatively to re-form what religious bodies understand about their place and purpose in society...which is completely in keeping with the openly socialist connections of some of IWJ's key people. For example, John Sweeney, until recently the president of the American Federation of Labor-Congress of Industrial Organizations (AFL-CIO),[470] is a member of the Democratic Socialists of America[471] – which is also a supporter of the Employee Free Choice Act.[472]

As for the IWJ, the Democratic Socialists of America website is not only linked to it but the DSA has honored Bobo's work. She has been a Debs-Thomas-Harrington dinner honoree and was a 2010 Keynote speaker for the Atlanta DSA Douglass-Debs Dinner.[473] Her talk at that dinner gave a good bit of insight into IWJ's use of religious institutions. According to the DSA report of the evening, "the substance of Bobo's message was that religions organizations are a pervasive part of American social life. Over 50% of people attend weekly religious services and most religious social justice agenda's are more or less compatible

---

[470] AFL-CIO website, "AFL-CIO Officers Emeritus: John J. Sweeney: John J. Sweeney, President, 1995-2009:"
www.aflcio.org/aboutus/thisistheaflcio/leaders/officers_sweeney.cfm
[471] Social Democrats, USA, "About Us:"
www.socialdemocratsusa.org/aboutus.shtml
[472] David Green, "The Employee Free Choice Act – A DSA Priority," *Democratic Left* (a publication of DSA), Spring 2007.
[473] dsalaborblogmoderator post, "Kim Bobo to Keynote Atlanta DSA Douglass-Debs Dinner," Talking Union, 10-11-10.

with that of DSA."[474]

ALLIANCE FOR A JUST SOCIETY (FORMERLY THE NORTHWEST FEDERATION OF COMMUNITY ORGANIZATIONS)

Another national network[475] that is under the influence of the Midwest Academy is the Alliance for a Just Society.[476] Until late 2010, the organization was a *regional* entity of four affiliates called Northwest Federation of Community Organizations (NWFCO).[477] Formed in 1993, NWFCO coordinated the Health Rights Organizing Project[478] and, in 2008, the Main Street Alliance,[479] an association of small business coalitions that work together to influence pertinent public policy.[480] Both projects continue under the expanded Alliance.

The Alliance is autonomous but is itself part of the larger network of organizations allied with USAction (formerly Citizen

---

[474] Ron Baiman, "Debs Dinner 2001: A DSA Choral Event," *New Ground*, a publication of the Chicago Democratic Socialists of America, May-June 2001: www.chicagodsa.org/ngarchive/ng76.html

[475] The organizations are: Center for Intercultural Organizing, Colorado Progressive Coalition, Idaho Community Action Network, Indian People's Action (Montana), Maine People's Alliance, Make the Road New York, Montana Organizing Project, Oregon Action, Progressive Leadership Alliance of Nevada, and Washington Community Action Network

[476] www.idealist.org/view/org/Bfg7XDz5MPFP

[477] See, for example: Kevin Borden, NWFCO; Matt Haney, *Idaho Community Action Network;* and Renée Markus Hodin and Kim Shellenberger, *Community Catalyst,* "Don't Lien on Me: Why the State's Medical Indigency Care Program Is Unhealthy for Idahoans," *Idaho Community Action Network - The Access Project, Community Catalyst,* 2001.

[478] Health Rights Organizing Project: www.healthrightsproject.org

[479] Common Grant Application for the Northwest Federation of Community Organizations, 2007-2011.

[480] Main Street Alliance: www.mainstreetalliance.org

Action),[481] which was itself founded by Heather Booth, using Midwest Academy's training (see above). Therefore, one expects the Alliance for a Just Society – and NWFCO – to tout a strong, progressive political perspective concerning the three primary issues– health care, economic justice, and immigration and, it does:

> NWFCO exists to advance a progressive national agenda by executing regional and national campaigns for economic, racial and social equity and by building strong affiliates.[482]

The Alliance continues in the same vein:

> Building on the proven community organizing success of the Northwest Federation of Community Organizations (NWFCO), Alliance staff and partners set out not only to replicate on a national level the best of NWFCO's 17 years of praxis, but also to create a progressive infrastructure capable of meeting 21st century challenges to the American dream of liberty and justice for all.[483]

Building networks, therefore, is an important strategy for accomplishing the "progressive agenda." For instance, NWFCO was a member of the Western States Center and five of the eight

---

[481] List of USAction Support Affiliates:
www.usaction.org/site/pp.asp.206.html
[482] www.nwfco.org/who.htm
[483] Alliance for a Just Society website, Mission and Values:
allianceforajustsociety.org/about/mission-and-values

Alliance affiliates are Western State Center "communities."[484]

Prior to its founding in 1987, the Western States Center saw that:

> … progressive organizations and leaders were often working in isolation from one another serving particular constituencies or advancing specific issues.
>
> Scattered across a broad geographic area, they lacked resources, appropriate training programs, and mechanisms to share intelligence, plan strategies and spread successes. Opportunities to work together and increase their impact and effectiveness were often missed and national progressive funders and organizations often failed to understand and support the West. The right wing was gaining strength and important political ground while many progressives seemed disengaged from electoral efforts and disconnected from each other.
>
> In response to this set of circumstances, the Center was established to help strengthen and further develop the progressive movement in the West. For more than two decades, Western States Center has served to connect Western activists, building our sense of shared values,

---

[484] Western States Center website: www.westernstatescenter.org/our-communities/regional. Even after the formation of the Alliance, the Western States Center continued to claim NWFCO as a regional partner. There was no mention of Alliance for a Just Society, though Kayse Jama, a former trainer/organizer at the Western States Center is an Alliance Board member.

honing our strategies for building power, sharpening our political analyses, and forging relationships and alliances with the broader movement for social, economic, racial and environmental justice.[485]

Western States Center includes, as part of the progressive agenda, a Gender Justice Program. The Gender Justice Program's several initiatives address:

...sexism, heterosexism, transgender oppression, reproductive justice, and family security in the context of racial and economic justice. We use a movement-building approach to strengthen the capacity of organizations dedicated to LGBTQ equality, reproductive justice, and family security.[486]

"Reproductive justice" is a term for universal abortion "rights." Therefore, it comes as no surprise to find that the Western States Center is allied in various ways with the pro-abortion movement as, for example, in staff and board members who also serve Asian Communities for Reproductive Justice.[487]

---

[485] www.westernstatescenter.org/about/our-history-1
[486] www.westernstatescenter.org/our-work/gender-justice
[487] Moria Bowman, Director of the Gender Justice Program at Western States Center is the Asian Communities for Reproductive Justice EMERJ (Expanding the Movement for Empowerment and Reproductive Justice) Movement Building Director; Daniel Martinez HoSang is on the Board of Directors for both Alliance for a Just Society and the Asian Communities for Reproductive Justice: *reproductivejustice.org/staff-and-board.* The Asian Communities for Reproductive Justice is very explicit that its advocacy on behalf of "reproductive justice" is to make abortion universally "available"

NATIONAL PEOPLE'S ACTION - NATIONAL TRAINING AND
INFORMATION CENTER (NTIC) OF NATIONAL PEOPLE'S ACTION
(NPA).

National People's Action (NPA – formerly National People's
Action on Housing[488]) is a coalition of activist groups around the
United States[489] co-founded in 1972 by Gale Cincotta and Shel
Trapp.[490] Its policy, research, and training institute, the
National Training and Information Center (NTIC) was
established by them the same year.[491] Cincotta was Executive
Director of the NTIC from 1973-2001 and has been on the NPA
board from its inception;[492] Trapp was NTIC's national
coordinator[493]and NPA's organizing director (and later a board

---

(both in the sense of affordability to poor people and in the sense of easier
access to abortion clinics in poor neighborhoods):
reproductivejustice.org/what-is-reproductive-justice.
[488] Shel Trapp, "Dynamics of Organizing: In a series on Organizing and
Neighborhood Preservation," National Training and Information Center,
1976.
[489] National People's Action, Network members: www.npa-
us.org/index.php?option=com_content&task=view&id=177&Itemid=177
[490] Gale Cincotta, "From Redlining to Reinvestment: The Need for Eternal
Vigilance," Keynote speech
at 4th International Conference on Financial Services: "European Monetary
Union and the Regional
Responsibility of Financial Institutions Toward the Customer," Strasbourg,
France (European
Parliament), 9-27-96: www.iff-
hamburg.de/Strasburg_virtuell/Reden/cincotta.htm (accessed 3-25-97).
[491] National Training and Information Center, old website: www.ntic-us.org
[492] "From Redlining to Reinvestment…"
[493] "Dynamics of Organizing…" Other sources refer to him as NTIC's "staff
director" and "chief trainer."

member) until 2000.[494]

Trapp, a Methodist minister who acquired his taste for activism during the civil rights movement of the 1960s, attended a seminar led by the Alinsky-trained organizer Tom Gaudette and later helped Gaudette run the Chicago-based Organization for a Better Austin.[495] Cincotta, also trained by Gaudette,[496] became Organization for a Better Austin's president.[497]

The duo's most significant "victory" was the writing and passage of the federal Community Reinvestment Act, requiring financial institutions to lend money in "risky" communities.[498] The legislation banned banks from alleged "red-lining" practices, that is, from "discriminatorily" denying loans across the board in particular low-income areas rather than accessing people on their individual credit histories.[499]

Critics of the CRA point out that this change in lending practice made it increasingly difficult to appraise individual credit …and was therefore more risky than responsible. Even taking into account the liberal lending patterns of the time, substantial increases in home-purchase loans – a whopping 43%

---

[494] Margaret Ramirez, "Shel Trapp, 1935-2010: Community organizer, co-founder of National People's Action," *Chicago Tribune*, 10-25-10.

[495] "Shel Trapp, 1935-2010…"

[496] Loyola Marymount University (Los Angeles), William H. Hannon Library, The Thomas and Dorothy Leavey Center for the Study of Los Angeles Research Collection, Gaudette Biography: www.lmu.edu/Page5494.aspx

[497] Patrick Barry, "Heather Booth and Gale Cincotta: from grass-roots troublemakers to national leaders," *Illinois Issues,* January 1989.

[498] "From Redlining to Reinvestment…" Cincotta calls it the "CRA of 1976." More precisely, however, in 1976 the Housing and Mortgage Disclosure Act was passed which generated the data upon which the CRA was lobbied, and then passed, in 1977.

[499] Several subsequent studies challenge the analysis on which the CRA was predicated.

increase in low-income neighborhoods – meant that poorly qualified people acquired loans they couldn't manage. Furthermore, as the risk of lending increased, smaller lenders were unable to compete and were driven from poor neighborhoods entirely.[500]

Another aspect of the CRA was its provision that banks were required to keep loan records available to community organizations for scrutiny.

> As written, the CRA provided that when a bank appeared before regulatory agencies the community organizers had a right to testify about the bank's fulfillment of its duty to serve the needs of the community in which it operates. This enabled the community organizers to extort large donations from banks. If a bank wanted to undertake any new action, it knew that it would have to pay off the community organizers to get the request approved by the regulators. [501]

Over the decades, NPA has remained intensely committed to increased banking regulation. As a member of Heather Booth's Americans for Financial Reform, NPA joined Paul Booth's AFSCME union, Heather Booth's USAction, the Alinskyian organizing network PICO, and scores of additional progressive organizations[502] in "fighting to regulate the financial industry."[503]

---

[500] Michelle Minton, "The Community Reinvestment Act's Harmful Legacy: How It Hampers Access to Credit," Competitive Enterprise Institute, 3-20-08.

[501] Thayer Watkins, "The Community Reinvestment Act (CRA) of 1977: Red Lining," San Jose State University Department of Economics, undated.

[502] Americans for Financial Security, coalition members: ourfinancialsecurity.org

Under the banner of "Showdown on Wall Street," NPA – again working in coalition with the AFL-CIO – orchestrated protests in New York City.[504]

A year later, NPA's "Make Wall Street Pay" campaign included the takeover of a DC branch of Bank of America – and involved PICO and the Alliance for a Just Society.[505] Around the same time, ACORN's founder Wade Rathke announced there would be "days of rage in ten cities around JP Morgan Chase" that would be "the beginning of the anti-banking jihad." ACORN's campaign was organized by Paul Booth's SEIU union. Stephen Lerner of SEIU urged participants at the 2011 Left Forum "to do everything in their power to make the nation's financial problems far, far worse," including staying in their homes as long as possible without paying delinquent mortgages.[506]

Another effort to disrupt the economy, called "New Bottom Line," which called for participants to move as much money as possible out of major banks on November 5, 2011, was led by the same group, specifically NPA, PICO, the Industrial Areas

---

[503] Heather Booth bio, New Organizing Institute Staff: www.neworganizing.com/profile/Heather-Booth

[504] Showdown on Wall Street, 4-29-10: showdowninamerica.org/showdown-wall-street

[505] Make Wall Street Pay Press Release, "Homeowners Tell Attorneys General: 'Not Enough;' Hundreds Go to National Association of Attorneys General's Convention," 3-7-11: makewallstreetpay.org/news/2011_0307c.html; David Dayen, "National People's Action Takes over BofA Branch in DC: Updates, 3-7-11: news.firedoglake.com/2011/03/07/national-peoples-action-takes-over-bofa-branch-in-dc

[506] F. Vincent Vernuccio and Matthew Vadum, "SEIU plans days of rage against Wall Street: Boycotts, Marches, and Protests…How to Put Banks on the Edge of Insolvency," *Canada Free Press,* 7-18-11.

Foundation of the Southeast (IAF-SE), and others related to the former ACORN network. [507]

Although the Center for Community Change (CCC) isn't a community organizing network, *per se,* it has served as a significant funding agent for the Alinskyian networks. CCC began as a creation of the Ford Foundation in 1968, with $3.5 M in seed money, to provide its Community Development Corporation program with technical assistance. [508]

In the years of the Carter administration, federal money reached various progressive organizations via tax-exempt non-profits. "Many utopian organizations obtained money simultaneously from a variety of federal agencies....The Center of Community Change, creator of the Youth Project," which the authors of Coercive Utopians called a "funnel for tax exempt money to go to radical groups, many of them not tax-exempt." CCC received approximately $2 million from the Department of Labor, $600,000 from the Community Service Administration, over $600,000 from the Department of Housing and Urban Development and just under $1 ½ million from the Department of Justice. [509]

To garner more money from foundations, several organizations created the National Committee for Responsible Philanthropy. "The 'donee group,' as the National Committee

---

[507] "Hundreds Protest Wells Fargo Shareholder Meeting in SF," *San Francisco Bay Guardian* (online), 5-4-11; Joel B. Pollak, "Email from Lisa Fithian to Occupy Wall Street Confirms ACORN Role in Occupy's Next Assault on Banks," [undated but around 10-21-11].

[508] *Who Rules America? ...*

[509] Rael Jean Isaac & Erich Isaac, *The Coercive Utopians: Social Deception by America's Power Players*, Discipleship Books (Regnery Gateway, Inc), 1985, pp 187; 189.

for Responsible Philanthropy was originally known, was composed of a number of leaders of utopian organizations," among them Pablo Eisenberg, then president of the Center for Community Change. "The donee group demanded the government take over total responsibility for the charitable functions presently supported by foundations," with the role of private philanthropy being "to challenge existing institutions."[510] CCC acquires the money it distributes largely from foundations.[511]

> ...Take the Center for Community Change in Washington, DC, for example. In 2002, the center received $1.9 million from the Stewart Mott Foundation, along with $825,000 from the Ford Foundation, $751,000 from the Mary Reynolds Babcock Foundation, $630,000 from the Annie E. Casey Foundation, $290,000 from the Rosenberg Foundation, $225,000 from the Nathan Cummings Foundation, $200,000 from the Rockefeller Foundation, and $200,000 from the Open Society Institute, plus another $818,000 from 11 other foundations, for a total of $5.8 million.[512]

CCC's political work has always been – and remains –

---

[510] *Coercive Utopians* ...P 206-7

[511] *Who Rules America?* ...Domhoff writes that in 2002 CCC received nearly $6 M, including $200,000 from George Soros Open Society Institute, $1.9 M from the Stewart-Mott Foundation, $825,000 from the Ford Foundation, etc.

[512] *Who Rules America*..."The Ford Foundation in the Inner City: Forging an Alliance with Neighborhood Activists."

openly and unabashedly progressive. For example, its
Movement Vision Project explains itself as an effort to infuse the
progressive movement with "a coherent, common vision – one
that represents our values and dreams for America."[513] These
values include a pro-abortion position and the Center's
executive director Deepak Bhargava has stated quite openly on
its website that it's fighting for "lifting restrictions on women's
access to health services:"

> Even as we continue to fight for affordability, for
> a public option, for greater efforts on racial
> disparities, for lifting restrictions on women's
> access to health services and immigrant inclusion,
> we believe it is important for all Americans to
> take stock of the truly important changes that the
> current reform will achieve. [514]

This position is expressed in the Introduction to a special
project of the *Center,* its *Movement Vision Project*:

> The challenge posed by the lessons from the right
> is not just for individual, single-issue movements
> to articulate a shared vision but for those visions
> to add up to something even larger: a broader,
> multi-issue progressive movement. If related
> single-issue organizations working toward the
> same long-term goals would be more powerful,
> imagine the power of even more organizations,

---

[513] Center for Community Change, "An Introduction to the Movement Vision
Project:" www.cccfiles.org/issues/movementvision (accessed 2-1-10).
[514] Deepak Bhargava, Center for Community Change Blog, "Time to Cross
the Finish Line on Health Care Reform," 12-22-09
www.communitychange.org/blog/time-to-cross-the-finish-line-on-health-
care/view (accessed 1-26-10)

working across issues for the same ends.
Certainly the issues are intersectional – foreign
policy is inextricably intertwined with economic
development policy; abortion rights and
reproductive freedom intersect with criminal
justice. Our solutions must intersect as well.[515]

The CCC's resource library recommends an activists' guide
to promoting abortion rights, *Reproductive Justice Briefing Book: A
Primer on Reproductive Justice and Social Change* by SisterSong. The
CCC summary for the book says:

Need a one-stop shop for information on
reproductive justice? Well, SisterSong has got the
right tool for you. This series of articles
documents the struggle for reproductive justice
and bridges this struggle with other issues within
the social justice movement such as immigration
and queer rights. Additionally, the series touches
upon the future of the women's movement in
relation to reproductive justice.

CCC's progressive political activism is a bigger problem than
one might think at first glance. As an organization, it
"strengthens, connects and mobilizes grassroots groups to
enhance their leadership, voice and power."[516] These grassroots
groups include Alinskyian organizing networks, deeply

---

[515] "Introduction to the Movement Vision Project of the Center for
Community Change," as quoted in "Momentum Briefing – Visions and
Values: Articulating a Progressive Morality," a publication of the Tides
Foundation, Funding Strategy Two: Connecting the Dots.
[516] www.communitychange.org/who-we-are (accessed 7-29-10)

ensconced in Catholic parishes around the country and lured
into consensus-building for progressive ends:

> One of the Center's key strategies for making
> social justice part of policy debates is to build a
> unified agenda among its four core constituencies
> – African Americans, Native Americans, new
> immigrants, and low-wage whites – as part of its
> Campaign for Community Values.[517]

Under the banner of the Campaign for Community Values,
CCC co-sponsored a highly political and unabashedly partisan
conference with the Gamaliel Alinskyian community organizing
network. Called "Realizing the Promise: a Forum on
Community, Faith and Democracy," promotional material
boasted that, "As members of Congress, members of the
incoming [Obama] administration and our allies join us in
Washington, we will demonstrate the power of community
organizing to shape an inclusive and just policy agenda for
2009." [518]

Part of that agenda involves immigration activism that is
coordinated through the Fair Immigration Reform Movement
(FIRM), a national network founded by CCC that is comprised
of 300 organizations. Among these are several of the Alinskyian
community organizing networks, including the Gamaliel
Foundation, which identifies itself as "a major partner of

---

[517] [emphasis added] Independent Sector, 2008 American Express Building
Leadership Award, "IS to Present the Center for Community Change with
the 2008 American Express Building Leadership Award," 8-12-08
www.independentsector.org/istopresentthecenterforcommunitychangewitht
he2008americanexpressbuildingleadershipaward
[518] Gamaliel Foundation and Center for Community Change co-sponsored
flier for the 12-4-2008 event.

FIRM,"[519] and the National People's Action, which identifies itself as "an active member of the FIRM steering committee."[520] Additionally, affiliates of USAction, the Interfaith Worker Justice and the Alliance for a Just Society (specifically all the affiliates of the former Northwest Federation of Community Organizations) are members of FIRM's Immigrant Organizing Committee.[521] FIRM has been "integral to the coordination of the massive immigrant rights marches in 2006," conducting "12 'Democracy Schools' in Arizona, California, Idaho, Michigan, and Tennessee to assist immigrants with the citizenship process while identifying and training new immigrant community leaders."[522]

New community organizers are recruited through CCC's Generation Change project and its Youth Changing a Nation (YouthCAN), targets immigrant youth under age 25 to run "nonprofit organizations committed to important social change issues. YouthCAN has brought together young people from across the country to build strategy for winning critical legislation such as the DREAM Act."[523]

---

[519] MICAH (affiliate of Gamaliel), Immigration Task Force: www.micahempowers.org/immigration.html

[520] National People's Action, Immigrant Justice: webcache.googleusercontent.com/search?q=cache:dvP7BMSQ1LAJ:www.npa-us.org/index.php%3Foption%3Dcom_content%26task%3Dcategory%26sectionid%3D5%26id%3D29+%22Fair+Immigration+Reform+Movement+%22+%22National+People%27s+Action%22&cd=1&hl=en&ct=clnk&gl=us&client=firefox-a ; the FIRM website www.standing-firm.com/who-we-are lists NPA's National Training and Information Center as part of its Immigrant Organizing Committee…as well as the Gamaliel Foundation (accessed 4-19-11)

[521] FIRM website: www.standing-firm.com/who-we-are (accessed 4-19-11).

[522] "IS to Present the Center for Community Change…"

[523] "IS to Present the Center for Community Change…"

Even more to the point, ACORN, the Gamaliel Foundation and various Gamaliel affiliates consider themselves to be "partners" of CCC.[524] DART, Midwest Academy, RCNO, and NPA are engaged with CCC, as well.[525] Where CCC once merely provided technical assistance to various local community organizations, under the leadership of former ACORN organizer Deepak Bhargava "it has become in one organizer's words a 'political machine' – that is, has begun to amalgamate organizations' local capacity in nationally coordinated campaigns…"[526] PICO and Interfaith Worker Justice worked with the Gamaliel and the Center to push health care reform, despite its abortion components, and several PICO affiliates are CCC "partners."[527] And, as a further connection, Heather

---

[524] www.communitychange.org/who-we-are/our-partners In addition to the Gamaliel Foundation, Gamaliel affiliates that have been identified as CCC partners are: Gamaliel of Michigan, MOSES, AMOS, ABLE (a Gamaliel/IAF collaborative), ARISE, Empower Hampton Roads, Hopeful City, Genesis, Justice Overcoming Boundaries, CAUSE, and FACE.
[525] Center for Community Change: www.communitychange.org/COLIST.htm (accessed 10-10-02)
[526] Heidi Swarts, *Organizing Urban America: Secular and Faith-based Progressive Movements,* University of Minnesota press, 2008, p 186.
[527] PICO affiliates that have been identified as CCC partners are: Interfaith Action (NY), Queens Congregations United for Action, Congregations Building Community, and Metropolitan Organization for People (MOP). Another IAF collaborative (with OLTC and PICO), MCAN-Brockton Interfaith in Massachusetts, is also a CCC partner. Health Care for America Now website, "Who We Are" listing of coalition members: healthcareforamericanow.org/site/content/who_we_are . The HCAN coalition included the Planned Parenthood of America Federation, as well as ACORN, USAction, the Center for Community Change, Northwest Federation of Community Organizations, and Jobs for Justice (Interfaith Worker Justice), along with local affiliates of these groups; We Believe Together – Health Care for All website (inactive), Endorsing Organizations list: data.rac.org/bt/?page_id=2 identified a coalition that included the PICO National Network, Sojourners, Catholics in Alliance for the Common

Booth, co-founder of the Midwest Academy and USAction sits on CCC's board.[528]

NATIONAL COUNCIL OF LA RAZA

The National Council of La Raza is a development of Saul Alinsky's work in California among the Mexican Americans, where Alinsky and Fred Ross – an organizer trained by Alinsky's Industrial Areas Foundation – formed the Community Service Organization (CSO) in 1947. CSO, assisted by the IAF, grew to have a national staff and became the training ground for a number of prominent "Hispanic" organizers, among them Cesar Chavez, Dolores Huerta, and Herman Gallegos, first president of CSO's San Jose chapter and later CSO's national president.

Gallegos stayed with CSO until the early 60s and then went on to become a consultant at the Ford Foundation, which in 1968 funded the creation of the Southwest Council of La Raza (SCLR), whose founding president was Herman Gallegos. Ford created the SCLR to be "an intermediary organization between Ford and the barrio-based organizations," allowing for some distance between Foundation grants – and later, United States government grants – and local organizations with activities that "might be regarded as political."[529]

It took several years to determine exactly what SCLR's goals

Good, Gamaliel, Center for Community Change, and the Religious Coalition for Reproductive Choice.

[528] Center for Community Change: Board of Directors: www.communitychange.org/page/board (accessed 11-0-11)

[529] Herman E. Gallegos, "Equity and Diversity: Hispanics in the Non-Profit World," an oral history conducted in 1988 by Gabrielle Morris, the Regional Oral History Office, The Bancroft Library, University of California, Berkeley, 1989. Pp 67-69.

were. Gallegos felt "the community" wanted funding for "changes in institutions," while the Ford Foundation was looking for projects that could be measured concretely, in terms of housing units or jobs. A split was inevitable, with Gallegos going his way in 1970 and the SCLR becoming the *National Council of La Raza* (NCLR) in 1972 under new leadership and with lots of foundation money. Raul Yzaguirre served as NCLR's second president from 1974 to 2004.[530]

Raul Yzaguirre remained in a top leadership position with NCLR for over 30 years, shaping its public policies, more inflammatory rhetorically than in deed. Yzaguirre is reported, for example, to have said, "US English is to Hispanics as the Ku Klux Klan is to blacks." However, a NCLR "English-Only Fact Check" challenges the perception that Spanish-language immigrants don't learn English, and another NCLR publication, "Educating English Language Learners: Implementing Instructional Practices," describes strategies for developing English proficiency in a student who's native in another language. Evidently learning English isn't quite as deadly as Yzaguirre claimed.

NCLR's position on undocumented workers follows the general progressive line. "NCLR supports comprehensive immigration reform that includes the following principles," it says on the NCLR website,[531] which boil down to wanting legal status (amnesty) for the undocumented people already here – and putting them on the road to citizenship – and "unclogged" legal channels for future workers to immigrate into the country.

---

[530] "Equity and Diversity…," p 73;
[531] *Entire policy can be read at:* www.nclr.org/content/policy/detail/1058/

INTER-VALLEY PROJECT (IVP)

Kenneth Galdston, the director and organizer for the Inter-Valley Project (IVP) network, trained and worked with the Industrial Areas Foundation for seven years. [532]

The IVP network was formalized in 1997 with Galdston hired as its founding organizer. "Galdston had played a key role in the creation of each of these [founding] organizations, as the founding organizer of NVP [Nagatuck Valley Project] and MVP [Merrimack Valley Project], and as an advisor and supervising organizer in the creation of RIOP [Rhode Island Organizing Project] and PVP [Pioneer Valley Project], while serving as MVP Staff Director/Lead Organizer." [533]

IVP organizations are structured around a model it calls "democratic economic organizing" – elsewhere identified as "community economic empowerment. [IVP's] regional organizations of congregations, labor union locals, community and tenant groups combine citizen organizing and democratic economic development strategies to save and create jobs, affordable housing and critical public services."[534]

REGIONAL COUNCIL OF NEIGHBORHOOD ORGANIZATIONS/ REGIONAL CONGREGATIONS AND NEIGHBORHOOD ORGANIZATIONS (RCNO)

Regional Congregations and Neighborhood Organizations Training Center (RCNO, originally Regional Council of Neighborhood Organizations) is one of the smaller faith-based networks in the Alinskyian style but is particularly focused on

---

[532] InterValley Project Staff bios: www.intervalleyproject.org/staff.html
[533] History of Inter-Valley Project: www.intervalleyproject.org/history.html
[534] The Inter-Valley Project: www.intervalleyproject.org

African-American churches. [535] It was founded in 1983 by Rev. Joseph M. Kakalec, S.J. [536]

> He was the "George Washington of the modern neighborhood movement," said Edward A. Schwartz, a former City Councilman and city housing director. In the 1970s, Schwartz said, neighborhood activism was considered reactionary and suspect. "Joe gave it moral leadership…"

> …[I]n the early 1970s, Father Kakalec became involved with the Jesuit social ministry in North Philadelphia. …That year, Schwartz established the Institute for the Study of Civic Values in Philadelphia. He and Father Kakalec joined forces in 1976 to found the Philadelphia Council of Neighborhood Organizations (PCNO). When the council held a convention that year, 1,000 people attended, Schwartz said, representing 100 community groups. [537]

The year before founding RCNO, Father Kakalec took a yearlong sabbatical at the Jesuit School of Theology in Berkeley, California[538] where the Alinskyian community organizing and a

---

[535] Craig McGarvey, "Civic Participation and the Promise of Democracy," Center for Religion and Civic Culture (University of Southern California) Report, 2004, pp 28, 43.

[536] Guidestar organization information: www2.guidestar.org/PartnerReport.aspx?partner=justgivews&ein=22-2590488

[537] Sally A. Downey, "Rev. Joseph Kakalec, 77, civic activist," *The Inquirer,* 8-30-07.

[538] "Rev. Joseph Kakalec…"

liberationist "social justice ministry" were a staple of the curriculum.[539]

RCNO's current CEO and National Director is Rev. Eugene Williams, a Baptist minister who is "concerned with making the connections between theology and community development and revitalization meaningful to a broad cross section of people." [540]

CHRISTIANS SUPPORTING COMMUNITY ORGANIZING / ORGANIZING TRAINING CENTER (CSCO)

Special organizing efforts have been made to specifically target "conservative" Christians and draw them into the Alinskyian fold through Christians Supporting Community Organizing (CSCO). CSCO describes itself as a "national attempt to change the relationship between the theologically conservative elements of the Protestant church and community organizing. …CSCO represents a historically unique attempt to challenge decades of thought, theology, and action that have predisposed Evangelicals, Pentecostals, Holiness, and other theologically conservative Christians to avoid political engagement, except on a narrow range of issues related to personal behavior (e.g. abortion, promiscuous sex, divorce, school prayer, etc.)."[541]

Marilyn Stranske, national organizer and one of CSCO's founders, attended a workshop on community organizing led by

---

[539] Laurene Conner , "Anonymous People at the Switching Points of the Ecclesiastical Apparatus" *Wanderer Forum Foundation Focus*, Spring/Summer, 1994.
[540] RCNO website, Rev. Eugene Williams biography: www.rcno.org/Eugene_bio.pdf
[541] Christians Supporting Community Organizing website: www.cscoweb.org/usc.html

the IAF-trained Mike Miller in 1990 at which she had a
"conversion experience." "She realized that her theology and
worldview had lacked an adequate understanding of institutions
and the use and abuse of power. She began to consider how
congregation-based community organizing might address these
lacks, not only within herself, but also within the parts of the
church in which she had spent her life." [542]

CSCO is unabashed about its efforts:

> Unlike many community organizers, CSCO
> members understand the language, traditions,
> and viewpoints of the theologically conservative
> parts of the church because they are from these
> faith perspectives. CSCO's purpose is to get
> these churches to become part of the community
> organizing movement. CSCO seeks to
> accomplish its purpose through local members
> who are organized in branches that encompass
> metropolitan areas. Branch members conduct
> individual meetings, workshops, and other
> educational activities aimed at pastors and lay
> leaders of their faith perspectives. Rather than
> creating its own network of community
> organizations, CSCO works to establish a base of
> relationships through which it promotes the ideas
> of congregation-based community organizing and
> encourages its churches to join existing
> congregation-based community organizations that
> are already in place in their communities. This is
> a unique effort because the individuals who
> participate in CSCO become the "evangelists" to

---

[542] www.cscoweb.org/usc.html; also Gary Delgado, *Organizing the Movement:
The Roots and Growth of ACORN,* (Temple University Press: 1986), p 33

their churches, denominations, ministerial alliances, and peers.[543]

---

[543] www.cscoweb.org/usc.html

8. Funding from Religious Institutions to Alinskyian Organizing

If, as Alinsky taught, worldly power has two forms – money and people – the organizer's exhortation to "follow the money" must be taken seriously. Where *do* the Alinskyian networks get their money?

According to a 2001 report from Interfaith Funders, religious congregations constitute 87% of most faith-based community organizations' membership. Breaking that down further, Catholics make up 33% and Baptists 16%. United Methodist, Lutheran, Episcopal, Presbyterian and United Church of Christ congregations are, collectively, another third and Church of God in Christ, Jewish and Unitarian Universalist congregations make up the rest. [544]

With that in mind, Alinskyian organizations are funded in a number of ways. Some, like ACORN, have developed sophisticated ways of tapping into government money. Most have developed long-term relationships with philanthropic foundations. *Faith-based* Alinskyian organizations, however, have a unique source of revenue. While they may also receive "seed money" for starting or expanding new organizing projects from secular foundations, most of their initial funding comes from grants associated with the particular religious bodies forming their membership. [545] Once established, the community organizations

---

[544] Mark R. Warren and Richard L. Wood, "Faith-based Community Organizing: The State of the Field," Interfaith Funders," 2001.

[545] Albuquerque Interfaith Budget Report for the year 1994 shows that the New Mexico IAF local requested, as of September 30, 1994: $58,000 from the CHD, $1,000 from the ELCA Rocky Mt. Lutheran Synod, $7,500 from the Evangelical Lutheran Church of America, $10,000 from the Franciscans, $7,500 from the Jewish Fund for Justice, $26,000 from the Needmor Fund, $4,875 from the

receive "dues" from member institutions – usually a percentage (1-2%) of each institution's income.[546] Specific projects of these Alinskyian organizations may receive additional foundation money or government money.[547]

The purpose of this next section is to examine some of these religious funding mechanisms.

THE CATHOLICS: CATHOLIC CAMPAIGN FOR HUMAN DEVELOPMENT

One of the first religious bodies to fund Alinskyian organizing *consistently* was the United States Catholic Church.[548] Monsignor

---

Presbyterian Church, $4,000 from the Presbyterian World Service, $500 from the Rio Grande Conference of the United Methodist Church, $6,000 from the Unitarian Universalist Association, and $2,000 from Victory Noll.

The Omaha Together One Community, and IAF local in Nebraska, received total pledges of $69,775 in 1994 from the United Methodist Ministries, the United Methodist Conference, the Campaign for Human Development, the ELCA, and the Episcopal Diocese of Nebraska, as well as small donations from the Servants of Mary, Sisters of Mercy, the American Lutherans and several other.   Figures were taken from a semi-annual OTOC report July 1, 1993 - February 28, 1994.

[546] Valley Interfaith, an IAF affiliate in Texas, dues are 2% [olgray.org/Willacy county churches.htm]; Amos, an IAF affiliate in Iowa, dues are 1% [www.amosiowa.org/node/14]. Both have $15,000 caps.

[547] Materials [www.miamipact.org/files/33887604.doc] from People Acting for Community Together (PACT), an affiliate of DART in Florida, state that it is funded in four ways:

   1) Membership dues from the participating congregations or organizations (5% of revenue)

   2) Investments / donations from individuals and small businesses (5% of revenue)

   3) Investments / donations from local corporations (15% of revenue)

   4) Grants from a variety of private foundations and religious denominations (75% of revenue)

[548] The structure of the Catholic Church can make it awkward to talk about the actions of its members. The Catholic Campaign of Human Development

Jack Egan, an Alinskyian trained priest from Chicago who served on the Industrial Areas Foundation (IAF) board, used an annual meeting of his Catholic Committee on Urban Ministry – held in Combermere, Canada in 1969 – to "put together the fundamentals for the Campaign for Human Development. We then met with Cardinal Dearden, president of the American bishops, and sold him on the program. Cardinal Dearden sold the other bishops."[549]

Cardinal Dearden was so successful that by the annual meeting of the National Conference of Catholic Bishops in November 1969, "a resolution was approved calling for the appointment of an ad hoc committee to develop a plan for a 'Bishops' Crusade Against Poverty.'" By the spring 1970 meeting, the bishops passed a proposal to "raise funds to fight poverty through a special collection to be launched in the Thanksgiving season" and called the collection the Campaign for Human Development, thereby linking it to Pope Paul VI's encyclical, *Populorum Progressio*

---

began as an initiative of the United States Catholic Conference (USCC), a national lay organization that was related to – but independent from – the United States bishops. The history of the USCC is studded with questionable actions and its various departments were brought under closer episcopal scrutiny (presumably) when it was merged with the bishops' own bureaucracies (the National Conference of Catholic Bishops) to form the United States Conference of Catholic Bishops (USCCB). These bureaucratic bodies are complicated creatures with highly circumscribed authority, so to say the "US Catholic Church funds Alinskyian organizing" is a bit misleading. That said, the majority of US bishops contribute to the Campaign.

[549] Quoting Monsignor Eagan, Margery Frisbie, *An Alley in Chicago: The Ministry of a City Priest*, Sheed & Ward (1991), chapter 22. When Msgr. Egan refers to Cardinal Dearden as "president of the American bishops," he means that he is president of the National Conference of Catholic Bishops. The Catholic bishops were told that Alinskyian organizing was needed to teach low-income, inner city "ethnic and African-American communities to work together on common problems." (G. Wlliam Domhoff, *Who Rules America?* University of California at Santa Cruz, 2005 [first edition, 1967]).

("On the Development of Peoples"). To further associate the collection with the idea that it was a response to poverty, the Campaign took another statement of Pope Paul VI as its slogan: "For God's sake…break the hellish circle of poverty."[550]

The collection was always about funding Alinskyian organizing, however. [551]

> There was no formal link between the Campaign for Human Development and the Industrial Areas Foundation [at the CHD's inception]; but the philosophy behind the newly established CHD had been influenced by key Catholic leaders who in turn had been influenced by Alinsky and the IAF. In fact, funding from the CHD over the years has often gone to broad based community organizations established with the support of the IAF. During his visit to Britain in 1990, Rev. Al LoPinto, then director of the Campaign for Human Development, explained that the Campaign had no formal commitment to the IAF and broad based community organising; however, they found the approach to be effective and the IAF organisers to be very professional.[552]

---

[550] Ann Dempsey Burke, *The Bishop Who Dared: A biography of Bishop Michael Ryan Dempsey*, Valkyrie Press (1978), p 103-4.

[551] Richard L. Wood, *Faith in Action: Religion, Race, and Democratic Organizing in America*, University of Chicago Press, 2002, p 322, n 3.

[552] The Committee for Community Relations of the Bishops' Conference of England and Wales, "Acting Together For Change," April 1997. British spellings retained. The Wanderer Forum Foundation Commentary on the Campaign for Human Development (1997) found that the IAF receives the largest percentage of CHD grants among its grantees. During the funding period of 1992-1997, the IAF received approximately 15% of the national CHD annual budget, approximately $6,466,500 in total.

The bishops, if they read their own documents, should have understood this. These documents said that the collection was for "…organized groups of white and minority people to develop economic strength *and political power* in their own communities," (emphasis added) specifically through projects such as voter registration and community organizations.[553]

> This longstanding commitment of religious institutions to community organizing represents a story that remains to be told in its full depth. Here I simply note that according to all the staff people I interviewed, the primary funders of community organizers over the last three decades have been the Catholic bishops' Campaign for Human Development and to a lesser extent, various Protestant funding agencies. Essentially all federal funding of community organizing was eliminated in the late 1970s and early 1980s; CHD funding has been particularly essential since that time, with $27,917,500 having been dispersed to the four faith-based organizing networks in 755 grants since 1981.[554]

It was *always* about political power. "[T]he organization and the selling to the bishops of the Campaign for Human

---

[553] National Conference of Catholic Bishops, "Resolution on the Crusade against Poverty," adopted November 14, 1969 and quoted in James Jennings, ed., "Daring to Seek Justice," USCC, 1986, p. 69.
[554] *"Faith in Action…,"* p 291-2; A note from Wood about this section says that it is taken from "internal 1981-99 data from the CHD." Figures, of course, are now much higher. The four networks being examined are the IAF, PICO, Gamaliel, and DART.

Development – all were an attempt to make available and find support for Alinsky's approach to community organizing," said David Finks, another priest (since laicized) who had been trained by Alinsky and was among those in Combermere who drafted the initial proposal for the CHD collection. [555]

An analysis[556] of Campaign for Human Development grants during the 1990s demonstrated that about 33% of its grants at the time went to Alinsky-style, faith-based community organizations sporting highly politicized, left-wing agendas. The ACORN network received approximately 5%, the Industrial Areas Foundation network approximately 16%, Gamaliel approximately 4%, DART approximately 2%, and PICO approximately 6% of the national CHD annual budget, with smaller networks of community organizations receiving approximately 19%. These figures, however, didn't include the dues paid by member churches, the money given to network affiliates through *local* Campaign for Human Development grants, nor the grants coming into the networks through other Catholic bodies.

There has also been substantial cross-pollination between CHD personnel and its Alinskyian grantees. For example, Father – now Monsignor – Marvin Mottet, executive director of CHD from 1978 – 1985, had earlier been a member of ACORN;[557] Monsignor Jack Eagan, one of the founding minds

---

[555] Lawrence J. Engel, "The Influence of Saul Alinsky on the Campaign for Human Development," Theological Studies, December 1998 – interview of Finks with the author (FN 150).

[556] Wanderer Forum Foundation 1997 *Commentary on the Campaign for Human Development*. Later analyses showed little change in the percentages.

[557] Rael Jean and Erich Isaac, "The Coercive Utopians: Social Deception by America's Power Players," (Discipleship Books (An Imprint of Regnery): 1985), p 210.

behind CHD, was a cofounder of Interfaith Worker Justice.[558]

Using donations given to "help the poor" to instead help power-seeking politicians attain their ends is pure Alinskyianism. One of Obama's Chicago mentors, Gregory Galluzzo - a former Jesuit priest, now married, and Executive Director of the Gamaliel community organizing network — was interviewed by a writer to whom he showed the training manual he uses with new organizers.

> Galluzzo told me that many new trainees have an aversion to Alinsky's gritty approach because they come to organizing as idealists rather than realists. But Galluzzo's manual instructs them to get over these hang-ups. "We are not virtuous by not wanting power," it says. "We are really cowards for not wanting power,' because 'power is good' and 'powerlessness is evil."[559]

Other analysts have identified a relationship between Alinskyian community organizing, C/CHD funding, and liberation theology — which makes sense, given the relationship between Alinskyian organizing and Catholic dissent. One writes: "The Campaign [for Human Development] is informed by a North American version of liberation theology heavily influenced by Alinsky." [560]

---

[558] Interfaith Worker Justice history: www.iwj.org/template/page.cfm?id=93

[559] National Public Radio, On the Media Transcript: "Everyone's Favorite Radical," 8-7-09. Interview of Ryan Lizza of *The New Yorker* by NPR's Bob Garfield.

[560] Heidi J. Swarts, Organizing Urban America: Secular and Faith-based Progressive Movements, University of Minnesota Press, 2008, p 5.

Was the C/CHD being intentionally duplicitous? It would seem so.

> Except within certain religious and activist circles, it is not widely known that the Church's Campaign for Human Development expends most of its $8 million annual budget in grants to community organizing and grassroots empowerment efforts. And many of the recipients of the CHD largesse are IAF-directed projects. [561]

Another writer, the Catholic-dissenter Charles Curran, wrote that the "CHD obviously does not want to call undue attention to the conflictual aspects that are by definition a part of its organizing the poor and powerless."[562] Even those within the Church hierarchy, the "professionals," Curran says, may not be aware of what is the CHD's primary mission.

Considering the years of advertising for this collection among the laity, one would have to ask *why* it is not widely known how the C/CHD expends most of its annual budget. One would guess that slogans such as "Break the hellish circle of poverty" have misled the faithful into believing their donations have been used in legitimate ways.

It should further be noted that, over the years, a good number of Catholic clergy have undergone training with the various Alinskyian organizing networks. While not exclusively targeting Catholic clergy, Gamaliel's 20th Annual National Clergy Caucus Training was held at the Catholic University of

---

[561] Sanford D. Horwitt, *Let Them Call Me Rebel,* (New York: Vintage Books, 1989), p 546.

[562.] Charles Curran, *Directions in Catholic Social Ethics,* (Indiana: University of Notre Dame, 1985), chapter on "Saul D. Alinsky, Catholic Social Practice, and Catholic Theory," p. 151.

St. Mary of the Lake, at Mundelein Seminary.[563]

THE EVANGELICALS AND THE BAPTISTS

In 1985, Rael Jean Isaac and Erich Isaac wrote a remarkable book called The Coercive Utopians: Social Deception by America's Power Players. It describes the movement of specific leftist political ideas throughout the various denominations of Christendom.

The Isaacs were careful to make the point that they are not chronicling a *conspiracy* but an *ideology* of people from "diverse backgrounds and traditions,"[564] who have concluded that capitalism is fundamentally flawed and are pursuing a common idealization of a perfected society based on restructured institutions.

> The coercive utopians make no secret that their aim is power....the favorite method of the utopians, in staking out power, is to establish a community action organization. Typically, they consist of a small group of activists representing at most tiny minorities who claim to be representing majorities. Their techniques are based on the late Saul Alinsky, on whose book, Rules for Radicals, all community organizers base

---

[563] Gamaliel, April 12-14, 2011 Conference Flier, "Holy Calling to Holy Work," and conference agenda. Gamaliel's national, week-long leadership training was held at the seminary a month earlier: Training Packet for March 13-19, 2011.
[564] Rael Jean Isaac and Erich Isaac, *The Coercive Utopians: Social Deception by America's Power Players*, Discipleship Books (Regnery Gateway, Inc.), 1985, p 5.

their campaigns.[565]

To accomplish the first step – power – the Alinskyian organizations rely heavily on government, church, and foundation funding. Catholic "charitable" funding – specifically through the Catholic Campaign for Human Development – and the dues from parish members provide a significant portion of this, but the Alinskyian organizations are *ecumenical*. Therefore, one finds similar funding, accompanied by similar theological distortions, among other religious bodies.

Leftist theology has its roots in the "social gospel" spread among certain Protestant groups in the late nineteenth century.[566] "Social gospel" adherents believed that God expects human beings to create the "Kingdom of Heaven" by ridding the world of poverty, racism, and other social evils. The Rockefeller-funded Federal Council of Churches, the precursor of the National Council of Churches, formerly embraced the "social gospel" in 1908 and, during the Great Depression, these ideas spread rapidly through various US Protestant denominations.[567]

In the activist, anti-war years of the mid twentieth century, the "social gospel" branched in several directions. In Baptist and

---

[565] *The Coercive Utopians*...p 166, 167-168.

[566] The "social gospel" was a development of the ideas of Baptist minister Walter Rauschenbusch, who worked among the poor of New York City. "Unlike nineteenth-century reformers who sought to help the poor by teaching them the bourgeois virtues of hard work, thrift, and diligence, Rauschenbusch believed that the best way to uplift the downtrodden was to redistribute society's wealth and forge an egalitarian society. In Christ's name, capitalism had to fall. 'The Kingdom of God is a collective conception,' Rauschenbusch wrote in *Christianity and the Social Crisis*, politicizing the Gospel's message. 'It is not a matter of getting individuals to heaven, but of transforming the life on earth into the harmony of heaven.'" Steven Malanga, "The Religious Left, Reborn," *City Journal*, Autumn 2007.

[567] *The Coercive Utopians*...p 35.

fundamentalist circles, its most lasting manifestation was in the 1973 formation of the Evangelicals for Social Action (ESA). [568] Its forty founding "evangelical leaders" issued the "Chicago Declaration of Evangelical Social Concern," arguing that the United States was beset with numerous evils:

> ...the materialism of our culture and the maldistribution of the nation's wealth and services.... the misplaced trust of the nation in economic and military might - a proud trust that promotes a national pathology of war and violence which victimizes our neighbors at home and abroad.....[and the encouragement of] men to prideful domination and women to irresponsible passivity. [569]

Rev. Jim Wallis was on the planning committee from which the ESA sprang. [570] Wallis is a writer and a progressive political activist who founded and edits *Sojourners* magazine and directs an organization by the same name. He is a non-denomination Evangelical Protestant minister.

In 1983, Sojourners co-created Witness for Peace Tours to generate pro-Sandinista (Marxist) support in the United States. United States delegates were taken to Nicaragua and treated to staged "pep rallies," supposedly demonstrating popular

---

[568] Evangelicals for Social Action website, About Us section, www.esa-online.org
[569] Evangelicals for Social Action, "Chicago Declaration of Evangelical Social Concern," November 25, 1973, Chicago, Illinois
[570] Billy Graham Center, Archives, "Evangelicals for Social Action - Collection 37," www.wheaton.edu/bgc/archives/GUIDES/037.htm

enthusiasm for the Sandinistas.[571]

Meanwhile, back home, *Sojourners* magazine wrote glowing articles about liberation theology's inroads into the spiritual life of Latin Americans,[572] portrayed the US military and US Latin American foreign policy as "anti-Christ,"[573] and claimed that US economic assistance went exclusively to countries that repress and torture their citizens.[574]

So Sojourners has always been interested in left-wing political causes. In anticipation of the 1996 elections, Wallis convened what was, at the time, called an "evangelical para-church political action group," Call to Renewal – Christians for a New Political Vision, "created out of the perceived need to present an alternative viewpoint to the dominant conservative political agenda – represented by such groups as the boards of Christian Coalition."[575] At one point, its literature described Call to Renewal as "an interfaith effort to end poverty" and during the summer of 2006 it merged boards with Sojourners.[576]

Call to Renewal partners and affiliates were a modest fellowship, comprised primarily of progressive protestant organizations and a handful of powerful Catholic groups.[577] In

---

[571] Edmund W. Robb and Julia Robb, *The Betrayal of the Church,* Crossway Books, 1986; Witness for Peace, Mission and History page, www.witnessforpeace.org.

[572] Joan Harris, *The Sojourners File*, New Century Foundation, 1983, pp 4-5.

[573] *The Sojourners File*…p 8-9, quoting *Sojourners,* July/August 1981, p 7.

[574] *The Sojourners File*…p 23-24, quoting *Sojourners,* June 1977, pp 3-4.

[575] University of Virginia, New Religious Movements: Call to Renewal - Christians for a New Political Vision, web.archive.org/web/20060830125446/religiousmovements.lib.virginia.ed u/nrms/Callrenu.html

[576] Sojourners, About Us, "The reunification of Sojourners and Call to Renewal," www.sojo.net/index.cfm?action=about_us.reunification

[577] Call to Renewal Network, Listing of Partners, Affiliates, and Collaborating Organizations: www.calltorenewal.com/network.cfm (accessed 10-7-01)

some instances, it described itself as politically "moderate."[578] "Moderate," was a rhetorical term meant to sooth anxieties about Call to Renewal's political activism. Wallis, who was the president of the radical Students for a Democratic Society (SDS) chapter of his college campus and a stout supporter of Alinskyian faith-based organizing, was certainly aware of the organizing adage: "You do what you can with what you have and clothe it with moral garments….all effective action requires the passport of morality." The bottom line, however, was that Call to Renewal was working to get progressive candidates in office.

In the face of the 2008 presidential elections, under the auspices of the Center for American Progress, Wallis and other progressive "faith leaders" began a more ambitious — and much more sophisticated —project, Faith in Public Life. The website for Faith in Public Life explained that its founding was sparked by the 2004 elections to support what it called the "social justice faith movement" and develop "increased and effective collaboration, coordination, and communication on the national, state and local level." In contrast to the "religious right," Faith in Public Life eschewed, according to its spokes-folk at the time, the issues of abortion and homosexuality to focus on "social and economic justice" — although many of its associate groups argue that abortion and homosexual rights *are* social and economic justice issues.[579]

CHRISTIANS SUPPORTING COMMUNITY ORGANIZING

"Social gospel" theology has also spawned support of community organizing through Christians Supporting

---

[578] Mark Tooley, "Sojourn to the Center: Has Religious-Left Activist Jim Wallis Gone Moderate?" *Touchstone Magazine*, April 2002.

[579] Chapter 34 discusses Faith in Public Life in more detail.

Community Organizing (CSCO), founded in 1997[580] by progressively-minded Evangelicals, Pentecostals, Baptists, and other "related Christian leaders." In explaining their work in this capacity, CSCO writes, "We are persuaded that local congregations of our faith perspectives should explore congregation-based community organizing as a means to faithfully live out the Gospel."[581]

CSCO's story begins, however, several years before its founding, when "Marilyn Stranske attended a workshop on community organizing led by Mike Miller and co-sponsored by World Vision International's Office of Urban Advance —then co-directed by Dr. Robert Linthicum—and the Bresee Institute."[582] Miller, founding executive director of ORGANIZE Training Center (OTC), had organized under Saul Alinsky in 1966, as a "staff director" for a Kansas City, Missouri, organizing project of the Industrial Areas Foundation.[583] Miller took that experience – and earlier work organizing for the civil rights movements – to create programs that provide "consulting, workshop, and training assistance" to community organizations and unions. CSCO was among them:

From 1993-1999, OTC was the principal

---

[580] 1997 is the founding date given at the CSCO website: www.cscoweb.org/brief.html; however, the CSCO member profile on the Colorado Association of Nonprofit Organizations website from 2001 says CSCO was founded/incorporated in 1994.

[581] Christians Supporting Community Organizing website, "Proclamation and Call to Our Churches, Preamble," www.cscoweb.org/proc.html

[582] Report on a study of CSCO by the *Center for Religion and Civic Culture,* "A New Voice for Change among Evangelical, Holiness and Pentecostal Christians," University of Southern California, 1999, www.cscoweb.org/usc.html#history.

[583] Veterans of the Civil Rights Movement, Mike Miller, "After SNCC...brief notes on what I've been up to since 1966," last modified 5-27-10, www.crmvet.org/vet/mikemill.htm

consultant to Christians Supporting Community
Organizing, a national effort aimed at involving
churches of Evangelical, Holiness, Pentecostal
and related faith perspectives in already existing
congregation-based community organizing
projects around the country that focus their
efforts on social and economic justice and
extending democracy to marginalized groups. [584]

Bob Linthicum, the other workshop co-sponsor and now a
CSCO "leader," created and directed World Vision
International's "Office of Urban Advance" for community
organizing in 1985. [585] He prepared a training curriculum,
"Biblical Foundations for Community Organizing," OTC's
California Project. "Interest in the Project's theological work
led IAF to contract with Linthicum to help train IAF leaders and
organizers throughout northern California, Oregon and
Washington. PICO organizers have enrolled in Project-
sponsored workshops."[586]

For her part, Marilyn Stranske, "began a period of directed
study with Miller, pursued an internship in congregation-based

[584] ORGANIZE Training Center, "About OTC,"
www.organizetrainingcenter.org/about.html.
[585] Robert Linthicum, "Doing Community Organizing in the Urban Slums of
India," Social Policy, 12-22-01; Dr Robert Linthicum official website:
www.rclinthicum@org
[586] David Scheie, with T Williams and Luisa Pessoa-Brandão, Organized
Religion and Civic Culture: Final Report from a Strategic Review," prepared
for The James Irvine Foundation, April 2001. (3/99 report, p.3, 3/98 report
attachment, Craig McGarvey comment in 1/01)

organizing in Denver,[587] and traveled to Asia with Linthicum as part of a delegation examining World Vision-supported congregation-based community organizing. Through this process Ms. Stranske discerned that she had a 'call' to connect Evangelical, Holiness, and Pentecostal churches to community organizing." Stranske did the legwork of gathering progressively-minded denominational church leaders and Miller conducted sessions on faith-based organizing for them.[588]

CSCO's founding "proclamation" says:

> We speak in the tradition of the great revivals of the 18th and 19th centuries when our predecessors led the struggle to: abolish slavery; create real neighborhoods to replace slum conditions that forced people to live in degrading poverty; end child labor, as well as other abuses of working people; and, extend the right to vote to women.

> We speak in the liberating tradition of the African-American church which has historically understood God's purpose to include community, justice and freedom. In this tradition, we stand with: the slaves whose Christianity embodied the prophetic voice of Israel and who reminded us that the City on the Hill was also Pharaoh's Egypt; the abolitionists who struggled to end slavery; and, the civil rights movement of the 20th century.

---

[587] As of 2010, Stranske is a community organizer with PICO affiliate in Denver, Metro Organizations for People: www.mopdenver.org/about?id=0002

[588] "A New Voice for Change among Evangelical, Holiness and Pentecostal Christians…"

> We speak in the tradition of the Azusa Street
> Pentecostal movement which: recognized the
> importance of community, and challenged a
> concept of individualism that affirmed human
> independence by denying our interdependence;
> broke barriers of race, ethnicity and gender by
> recognizing the uniqueness and gifts of all people;
> and, reaffirmed the presence and power of the
> Holy Spirit among us. In these traditions, to those
> who share them with us, we speak.[589]

CSCO is open about the tension between traditional
Christian thought and its own perspective, necessitating the
"CSCO Reflects" program to "develop a conceptual base" for
churches from evangelical and Baptist faith perspectives to
become involved in faith-based community organizing."[590]

> To make participation in congregation-based
> community organizing "thinkable," CSCO has
> developed a biblically-based theology. Our parts
> of the church share the centrality of Scripture.
> Although justice for the poor, the discriminated
> against and the marginalized is a major theme in
> the Bible, it nevertheless is too often neglected in
> our circles. CSCO continues to deepen the
> biblical, theological and historic bases for its
> action and makes on-going biblical reflection and

---

[589] Christians Supporting Community Organizing website,
www.cscoweb.org/about.html
[590] Christians Supporting Community Organizing website,
www.cscoweb.org/mile.html

study an integral part of its work.[591]

CSCO believes that most Christians in its circle "view their faith as a personal or private matter and view social problems as the result of failures of individual morality."

> One of the primary reasons [evangelicals haven't been involved in Alinskyian organizing] is that the theologically conservative elements of the church have focused their attention on individual salvation and personal faith, and have not emphasized the need for social action of this kind. Another factor has been the view that political involvement and the use of power are worldly concerns and are therefore inevitably corrupting influences with no redeeming virtues.[592]

The CSCO statement is, of course, a Marxist construct. There's no such thing as being "theologically conservative." Either a dogmatic statement is true or it isn't.

Further, contrasting "individual salvation and personal faith" to "social action" is patently unjust. Most Christian communities are concerned with both, though they may understand "social action" as referring less to a generalized "doing good" than to the loving, personal, individual assistance of one person to a specific, irreplaceable brother created in the image and likeness of the personal God. CSCO, by contrast, tackles social problems through community organizing, holding government and private corporations "accountable."[593]

---

[591] Christians Supporting Community Organizing website, www.cscoweb.org/brief.html

[592] "A New Voice for Change among Evangelical, Holiness and Pentecostal Christians…"

[593] CSCO, www.cscoweb.org/brief.html

In California, "CSCO's work is done under the auspices of the California Project" and is directed by Miller. [594]

WORLD VISION INTERNATIONAL

The original World Vision was founded in 1950 by the evangelical missionary Rev. Dr. Robert Pierce to assist Asian orphans and other children in need, primarily through "child sponsorship" programs. Dr. Pierce headed World Vision until 1967. [595]

Today's organization, World Vision International (WVI) has expanded its work both geographically and ideologically. While it continues to provide some emergency relief, its primary focus is community development and advocacy. An evangelical-based development agency with staff in Africa, Asia and Latin America, WVI now considers community organizing "a major component of its work."[596]

The relationship of World Vision to community organizing has largely been shaped by the work of Robert (Bob) Linthicum, who created and directed its "Office of Urban Advance," dedicated to that purpose. Linthicum provides a striking example of his perspective:

> When I was directing World Vision's urban work outside the United States, we had the situation in Madras, India where the city government

---

[594] "A New Voice for Change among Evangelical, Holiness and Pentecostal Christians…"

[595] Tim Stafford, "Imperfect Instrument: World Vision's founder led a tragic and inspiring life," *Christianity Today*, 2-24-05

[596] Robert Linthicum, "Doing Community Organizing in the Urban Slums of India," Social Policy, 12-22-01.

rounded up all the untouchables living on the
streets of Madras and moved them to a
government-owned flood plain outside Madras
that was uninhabitable because of flooding twice a
year by monsoons. World Vision went in and
provided immediate relief. But I also sent my best
Indian organizers into the situation. There, they
got the people together into groups to work on
solving the complex and multiple problems of
building a new community upon that flood plain.
Now if World Vision had only been doing
community development at that time, it would
have decided it needed to mobilize the people to
build homes for themselves – and it would likely
have cost World Vision around $1,500,000 to
complete that project. Instead, we were
committed to doing community organizing. Our
organizers motivated the people to declare to
each other, "The government created the
problem by forcing us to move here. Let them
now solve the problem they created!" And those
untouchables organized themselves to confront
the government at every turn of the road
regarding this injustice. Eventually, they ended
up making their case, face-to-face, before the
governor of the state of Tamil Nadu (in which
Madras is located and to whom the city
government is accountable). The result is that not
only did the government build houses for every
family, but it sold the land and homes to the
people at an extremely low price, and the
government built the infrastructure of a floodwall
(to keep the monsoon floods out), paved the
streets, brought in electricity and plumbing, and

even built a school, library and community
center. The cost to the government was
$1,500,000, and the cost to World Vision for
three years of organizing and the salaries of five
full-time organizers was a total of $35,000![597]

It is this shift from assistance, in this case, "community
development," to *conscientizing* the needy – indoctrinating the
idea: "The government created the problem …Let them now
solve the problem they created!" – that critics find
disturbing…and not a little reminiscent of Saul Alinsky's ugly
"The hell with charity; the only thing you'll get is what you're
strong enough to get."[598]

This shift has generated serious confusion among World
Vision donors who are still under the illusion that their money
goes directly to children in need. Reporter Andrew Geoghegan
visited his World Vision sponsor child as part of a 2008 report[599]
about the ongoing Ethiopian famine and discovered that his
contributions hadn't gone to the child's family, despite
correspondence that he construed to indicate that it had.
Mentioning this fact briefly within the overall coverage of the
famine, World Vision responded:

> World Vision unapologetically takes a
> community-based approach to development – a

---

[597] Robert Linthicum, "What precisely is community organizing? How does it differ from community development?" Christians Supporting Community Organizing website, undate.

[598] Quoted in Dick Kirschten, "Campaign Chronicle: Not Having to Ask for Charity," *National Journal*, 3-19-88, p 760.

[599] Andrew Geoghegan, "Ethiopia - The Endless Famine," ABC Broadcast: 25-11-08 (SERIES 18, EPISODE 22)

fact we publicly promote at every opportunity. Providing money directly to the families of sponsored children simply does not work, no matter how dire the circumstances. A 'direct benefit' approach creates jealousy among community members that do not have sponsored children and fosters an ethos of dependency. So while sponsored children may receive some direct benefits – like school materials or a jacket for warmth – this in no way represents the entirety of our work in a community, and it was disingenuous for the Foreign Correspondent story to imply this.[600]

ORGANIZING AMONG PRESBYTERIANS AND LUTHERANS

The "social gospel" is alive and kicking among the mainstream Protestant denominations, as well. A recent example of this thought is echoed in a quote from Bishop Roy Dixon, prelate of the Southern California 4th ecclesiastical jurisdiction of the Church of God in Christ, a member of the San Diego Organizing Project, and former board chair of the PICO National Network (of which SDOP is an affiliate). Defending the work of community organizers, Dixon said, "When people come together in my church hall to improve our community, they're building the Kingdom of God in San Diego. We see the fruits of community organizing in safer streets, new parks, and new affordable housing."

There's a price to be paid for this new "gospel," however. Every denomination in which it has taken root, has experienced

---

[600] Tim Costello, "World Vision response to Foreign Correspondent story from Ethiopia broadcast on 25 November 2008," www.abc.net.au/foreign/World_Vision_Response.htm

a rift. The US Presbyterian Church, for example, is divided between the PCUSA – the Presbyterian Church in the United States of America – and more theologically conservative branches of the denomination.

In 2005, the PCUSA signed a joint statement with the Evangelical Lutheran Church of America to become more involved nationally with community organizing. It's a fascinating position paper, the product of a national gathering coordinated by the Urban Ministry Office of the Presbyterian Church (USA) and the Congregation-based Community Organizing/Leadership Development for Public Life Office of the Evangelical Lutheran Church in America.[601] It observes that congregation-based (faith-based) community organizing, already an established fact in many congregations, has "proven to be a revitalizing strategy for congregations and expands the reach and vision of ministry." It therefore advocates that each denomination increase funding for organizing and explore the ways it "can be a vital part of congregational re-development and new church development.... working together with other denominations on a national strategy around public policy using a community organizing framework."

For seminarians, there is the particular recommendation to "engage in appropriate learning projects related to congregation-based community organizing. Faculties of seminaries [should] be encouraged to provide resources to the larger church of the theological and biblical foundations of social justice through a CBCO [congregation-based community organizing] strategy."

Congregations are mandated to employ "the strategies of community organizing – individual meetings, house meetings,

---

[601] "Lutheran—Presbyterian Congregation-based Community Organizing Consultation," signed October 13-15, 2005, www.interfaithfunders.org/PresbandLutherans.html.

building a relational culture – for congregational transformation....[u]sing CBCO as a primary strategy for mission, understanding its systemic approach as compared to direct service or advocacy."

The Presbyterian Church has a history with community organizing. Organizer Fred Ross, born in California in 1910, was hired by Saul Alinsky in 1947 to help form the Community Service Organization (CSO, now defunct) in Los Angeles. Ross, in turn, trained and hired Cesar Chavez to work under him as a full-time CSO organizer. When Chavez quit the CSO in the early 1960s, Ross worked for the national Presbyterian Church, organizing Yaqui Indians near Tempe, Arizona.[602]

Funding for these efforts has come from several collections. The Presbyterian Hunger Program (PHP) in partnership with the Presbyterian Church (U.S.A.)'s Small Church and Community Ministry Office, regularly allocates grants to congregation-based community organizations within the Alinskyian networks.

> Grants are provided to support training for lay leaders, pastors, middle governing bodies, staff, and seminarians to develop the skills for congregational-based community organizing.
>
> ...The funds are from the Community Development portion of the One Great Hour of

---

[602] Material taken from the PICO website: "Axioms for Organizers," by Fred Ross, Sr., www.piconetwork.org/organizing/tools?id=0023 . Presbyterian are quite proud of this history: "The Presbyterian Church has been a catalyst in the evolution of this movement since its inception in the 1950s. The denomination has been one of the major funders nationally and hundreds of congregations have been involved at the grassroots level. (General Assembly Mission Council, Leadership Training and Scholarship Grants, gamc.pcusa.org/ministries/smallchurch/grants)

Sharing offering.

….."We'll use the grant to help pay for our
portion of the costs of sending people to get
trained," Stewart said. "We use it to help pay for
the salary and expenses of an organizer. We're all
volunteers in this except for the organizer, but in
order to do the work we want to do we have
costs."[603]

It's no secret that grants for congregational-based community
organizing through the major Alinskyian networks "is a strategy
for … developing individuals into effective leaders and change
agents."[604]

For its part, the liberal Evangelical Lutheran Church in
America (ELCA) was born in 1987, the product of various splits
and realignments among the US Lutheran population.[605] Almost
immediately after its inception, the ELCA began meeting with
members of the larger, national organizing networks. From
these discussions, the ELCA developed a six-point strategic plan
on the integration of faith-based organizing throughout the
denomination, hoping "to produce a powerful force that can act
as a real agent of social change."[606]

---

[603] Evan Silverstein, "Grants will support congregation-based community
programs," Presbyterian News Service, May 2, 2008
[604] General Assembly Mission Council, Leadership Training and Scholarship
Grants, gamc.pcusa.org/ministries/smallchurch/grants
[605] www.elca.org carries a detailed history
[606] www.faithinpubliclife.org/content/case-
studies/partnerships_between_national.html; The ELCA has a website for
those interested in its organizing efforts: www.elca.org/Our-Faith-In-
Action/Justice/Congregation-based-Organizing.aspx or
www2.elca.org/organizing/about

The four major Alinskyian networks are all involved in the project – the Industrial Areas Foundation, founded by Saul Alinsky, and DART, Gamaliel, and PICO, whose founding organizers learned their craft at Alinsky's feet. The "ultimate goal of this effort is to change the culture of the church so that community organizing is an integral part of every congregation of the ELCA."[607]

In an amazing display of self-service, the organizers help religious bodies to fund the secular community organization:

> Tony Aguilar, a former organizer for the Industrial Areas Foundation, is helping to refine the Evangelical Lutheran Church of America's philanthropic strategy. Aguilar serves as assistant to the bishop of the church's Metropolitan New York Synod…He is also coordinating the effort to set aside $2 million to $3 million that had been tied up in loans through the church's Dominion Hunger Fund to bankroll community development projects. [608]

It is hardly coincidental that at the same time the ELCA has been moving toward the goal of reinventing itself as an earthly "agent of social change," the denomination has been changing doctrinally, too. Official positions on homosexuality – expressing the traditional, Biblical belief that marriage is between a man and woman, that homosexual erotic activity is sinful, and that people leading homosexually active lives cannot hold positions of ministry – have been shifting over the last two

---

[607] www.faithinpubliclife.org/content/case-studies/partnerships_between_national.html
[608] Robert Neuwirth, "Faith and Philanthropy, Bridging the Secular and Sacred," NYRAGTIMES, Fall 2000.

decades. Naturally, the newly organized ELCA will bring its new moral values into the public – and political –arena.

In 2006, the ELCA Conference of Bishops "dedicated their annual Academy to training in congregation-based organizing" resulting in the authorization and funding of 3-day organizing "primers" to ELCA synods around the United States. These synodical trainings, called Vital Congregations: Just Communities (VCJC), are designed to equip leaders with the "biblical and theological components" for beginning involvement in community organizing.[609]

To fund community organizing efforts, the ELCA is using funds raised through its annual Hunger Appeal. In 2008, "a full 10% of the [Domestic Hunger Grants] awarded were for organizing initiatives, totaling $80,000 of Lutheran money going to 38 different projects."[610]

> Though we might hope for more ELCA Hunger dollars to go to organizing, and in fact that is a long-range goal, it's good to know that the percentage of organizing requests matched the percentage of awards granted. CBO Director Susan Engh is a member of the Domestic Hunger Grants allocation table. She found this, her first experience with the allocations process, to be quite beneficial, both in terms of the funds allocated for organizing and for the opportunity to further orient other team members to the world of organizing and its important role in the public church aspect of the ELCA's mission.

---

[609] Evangelical Lutheran Church in America CBO Newsletter, March, 2008
[610] Evangelical Lutheran Church in America CBO Newsletter, March, 2008

Susan also learned the importance of spreading the word, especially among organizing practitioners, that these ELCA Hunger dollars are indeed available for efforts that go beyond relief, direct services, and development, and into root-cause justice efforts. Those of us involved in organizing should continue to apply for these grants each year. When we receive these grants, we should make known the fact that our funding comes in part from the ELCA Hunger Appeal. And, we should encourage leaders and congregations to give generously to the Hunger Appeal, in order to grow these funds and thereby grow the amounts and percentages available for organizing. Ten percent is terrific, but imagine 30% or greater, coming from a fuller funding stream, in the coming years![611]

To further spread the new gospel of community organizing, a national Congregation-based Organizing Team (CBOT) serves the ELCA as a vehicle for bringing together ELCA church leaders participating in the various organizing networks. Pastors involved in DART, PICO, Gamaliel, and IAF affiliates are part of the CBOT team, overseeing such matters as Congregation Based Organizing Strategic Summits, Seminary Engagement in Congregation Based Organizing, First Call Theological Education and Congregation Based Organizing, and International Organizing.[612]

UNITED METHODISTS

---

[611] Evangelical Lutheran Church in America CBO Newsletter, March, 2008
[612] Evangelical Lutheran Church in America CBO Newsletter, March, 2008

There has certainly been widespread support for Alinskyian community organizing among other Protestant denominations, including their congregational membership in the various networks, but there has not been the same unified backing as found in the groups discussed above.

The United Methodists have had a particularly interesting history. Despite decades of support for extraordinarily left-wing causes,[613] there was division within the denomination over it. For example, the now defunct Alinskyian organization, the Rural Organizing Committee (ROC) in Holmes County Mississippi, "received core funding from the United Methodist Church for almost ten years." Comprised predominantly of "blacks," ROC was extremely successful in getting "black people into many elected and bureaucratic positions." As a result, they began to:

> …threaten the white power elite. Most of the elite were Methodists. Last year [late 1980s] the Methodist Church cut off funding to ROC and they have to lay off their full-time staff. Although some of them are continuing to work without money, they believe the whole project is in serious jeopardy. They had not foreseen this coming, even when the United Methodists began to fire all national staff that supported community organizing work.[614]

---

[613] An examination of the United Methodist's funding of radical left-wing groups, its exposure in the late 1970s by David Jessup, and subsequent actions to address the criticism raised can be read in *The Coercive Utopians.*

[614] Joan Newman Kuyek, *Fighting for Hope: Organizing to Realize Our Dreams,* Black Rose Books, 1990, p 166

That isn't to suggest United Methodist support for the Alinskyian networks has been inconsequential. For a number of years, Industrial Areas Foundation Regional Trainings have been held at the Drew University Theological School – "a theology school with Methodist roots and ecumenical concerns."[615] Drew seminarians have the fee waived if they attend the 5-day IAF training.[616]

Other seminaries operating out of the United Methodist tradition (but now "ecumenical") have been identified as "social justice" seminaries. In the fall 2010, Claremont School of Theology launched a School of Ethics, Politics, and Society connected to its School of Theology. "Master's of arts students can concentrate studies in community organizing (which includes courses on immigration and nonviolence) or inter-religious understanding. Either degree can emphasize peace and justice studies."[617]

At least one United Methodist bishop has had a rather substantial career in Alinskyian faith-based organizing. Since the 1980s, Minerva Carcaño, now Bishop of the Phoenix Episcopal Area of the United Methodist Southwest Conference, has been actively engaged with "community organizing ministry through the Industrial Areas Foundation."[618]

Some modest United Methodist grants are awarded to network affiliates. For example, a local "Justice Education and Leadership Development Program (JEALD)" was awarded

---

[615] www.drew.edu/history.aspx
[616] www.drew.edu/theo/cue.aspx?id=6007
[617] Kaitlin Barker, "More Social Justice Seminaries," *Sojourners Magazine*, September/October 2009.
[618] Virginia Armstrong, "Methodist Church Members Ask to Quit Valley Interfaith, Valley Morning Star, 10-28-84. The article describes Carcaño's church, El Divino Redentor Methodist of McAllen, Texas petitioning to withdraw from affiliation with the IAF-affiliate Valley Interfaith; Minerva G. Carcaño, Wikipedia entry

$12,000 for "a congregational effort to engage young adults in community organizing efforts through two Gamaliel Foundation organizing workshops, as well as restorative justice training. JEALD will address domestic violence prevention and juvenile offender ministries. The grant will be used to train five persons and provide peace with justice materials."[619] It's neither an enormous sum nor a large project but, over time, such investments yield dividends.

UNION FOR REFORM JUDAISM

The Jewish funding mechanism for Alinskyian organizing — Jewish Funds for Justice (JFSJ) — describes itself as a national public foundation "to combat the root causes of domestic social and economic injustice." To accomplish that, the JFSJ began a "national initiative" in 2002, to support congregation-based community organizing.

"Our goal was to address the lack of sustained engagement in activities beyond direct service programs and to challenge congregations to address systemic issues relating to domestic poverty and social injustice," the JFSJ website explains. Congregation-based community organizing "unites a diverse range of people, primarily through religious congregations, in the shared goal of building a civic power base capable of making change to promote the public good. Today, nearly 100 synagogues across the United States are engaged in or actively exploring CBCO."[620]

---

[619] United Methodist General Board of Church and Society, "United Methodist social justice agency awards $155,000 in Ethnic Local Church funding," 11-3-08.

[620] Jewish Funds for Justice website, "Congregation Based Community Organizing," www.jewishjustice.org/jfsj.php?page=2.5

The site reveals that "congregation-based community organizing" means something very specific to the JFSJ, namely membership in one of four Alinskyian organizing networks: Industrial Areas Foundation (IAF), PICO National Network (PICO), Direct Action Research and Training Center (DART), and the Gamaliel Foundation. In 2008, that's where JFSJ awarded a healthy percentage of its grants.

> Congregation-based organizing represents a paradigm shift, explains Rabbi Pesner. "Instead of asking, 'what can we do to help?' we ask, 'who has the power to change the situation?' Rather than asking, 'how much money can we raise to help adult children of congregants who don't have health insurance?' we ask, 'who has the power to make sure these young people are insured, why aren't they exercising this power now, and what can we do to convince them that change is necessary?'"[621]

Rabbi Jonah Pesner serves on JFSJ's Jewish Clergy Task Force.[622] He's also co-chair of the Boston Industrial Areas Foundation affiliate and also is the founding director of Just Congregations, a social action program developed by the Union of Reform Judaism and the JFSJ in 2006 to train Jewish congregations across the country in IAF-based organizing. Just Congregations provides the "language and organizing out of their faith tradition," as "the language of Christianity, in particular, can make Jews uncomfortable and hesitant to participate.

---

[621] Daniel David May, "Partners in Power," Reform Judaism Online, Spring 2009

[622] Before the 2008 presidential elections in the United States, Rabbi Jonah Presner was also a spokesman for *Faith in Public Life*, an organization that targets religious bodies with progressive political messages.

Exacerbating these feelings can be conflicting positions by the two faiths on issues such as abortion and gay rights."[623]

In addition to grants, Just Congregations and the JFSJ – which trains rabbinic and cantorial students in synagogue organizing through its Leadership for Public Life program – provide numerous resources supportive of Alinskyian organizing. According to Just Congregations literature, they recruit synagogue leaders for the national gathering, engage clergy in congregation-based community organizing task forces, connect leaders locally to JFSJ initiatives, and encourage seminary faculty and students to support and attend CBCO seminary training sessions. "[M]ost importantly, the Union/Just Congregations staff members would coordinate a national strategy together with JFSJ staff to determine together which geographic regions are ripe to be targeted for Reform Jewish engagement in CBCO."[624]

UNITARIAN UNIVERSALISTS

The Unitarian Universalist Association of Congregations (UUA or UU) is also on the congregation-based, community organizing bandwagon and published "Congregation-Based Community Organizing: A Social Justice Approach to Revitalizing Congregational Life" in 2006.

> This guide begins with a theological grounding
> for CBCO in pursuit of social justice and analyzes
> what prevents many contemporary Unitarian
> Universalists from being more assertively

---

[623] Daniel Levisohn, Assistant Editor, JTNews: "Faith Alliance reaches out to Jewish congregations," www.jtnews.net/index.php?/news/item/899
[624] urj.org/justcongregations/jfsj

engaged. The guide then describes how CBCO builds community, makes concrete changes to promote the public good, and develops community leaders. It describes the benefits reaped by participating congregations, including the building of interfaith, interclass, and interracial relationships; the addition of new congregational members; the development of leaders; and the new dynamism that transforms congregational life. The guide also analyzes the challenges to congregational participation in CBCO and the ways in which congregations can meet those challenges.[625]

The UUA guide also speaks of "shifting the paradigm." Its sense of "social justice" includes work, in its own words "for civil and human rights; for rights for gay men, lesbians, bisexuals, and transgendered people; for a healthier environment; for economic justice; and for peace and world community."[626] The tool for attaining long-term, "social justice" change is, of course, congregation-based community organization, and the guide mentions the major Alinskyian organizing networks, concluding:

> Congregation-based community organizing is an effective way to fulfill our mandate to work for a better world fully consistent with UU values, principles, and theology. Part of the mission of UU congregations is to move outside our walls and join in building bridges across the barriers

---

[625] www.uua.org/leaders/justice/cbco/27243.shtml

[626] Unitarian Universalist Association of Congregations, "Congregation-Based Community Organizing: A Social Justice Approach to Revitalizing Congregational Life," 2006.

that separate people from one another. It is the
work of restoring, creating, and maintaining right
relationships. Over a hundred of our fellowships
and churches are engaged with local network
affiliates, where they build multiclass, multirace,
and multifaith organizations through grass-roots
organizing. At the Unitarian Universalist
Association, we wish to encourage and expand
congregational participation in this movement. [627]

The Unitarian Universalist Funding Program provides grants
to community organizing through funds provided by the
Unitarian Universalist Veatch Program at Shelter Rock.
Specifically, its Fund for UU Social Responsibility "makes grants
to projects that increase UU involvement in social
responsibility," including a matching grants program for
Congregation-Based Community Organizing and the Fund for a
Just Society, which "makes grants to nonprofit organizations
addressing issues of social and economic justice. Grants are given
to projects that use community organizing to bring about
systemic change."[628]

INTERFAITH FUNDERS AND THE INTER-RELIGIOUS ORGANIZING
INITIATIVE

Just as embracing the "social gospel" has led to internal
denominational splits, it has created new alliances of people
across denominational lines. Interfaith Funders (IF) is one such

---

[627] "Congregation-Based Community Organizing…"
[628] Unitarlian Universalist Association of Congregations, "The Unitarian
Universalist Funding Program," undated,
www.uua.org/giving/fundingprogram

alliance — a "network of faith-based and secular grantmakers committed to social change and economic justice," but most specifically "to advance the field of congregation-based community organizing (CBCO, also known as Faith-based Community Organizing, FBCO)." [629]

Groups that have become members of Interfaith Funders are those that are most invested in congregation-based — Alinskyian — community organizing. [630] In addition to their own funding mechanisms, they are able to award "collaborative grants" through Interfaith Funders. One author, discussing "small, alternative funds, along with progressive religious funders," notes:

> Religious funders provided $26.3 million in grants in 1998. The Catholic Campaign for Human Development (CCHD) provided $14 million of the total, and the Unitarian Universalist Veatch Program at Shelter Rock provided $10 million. Interfaith Funders is a grantmaking consortium of 12 faith-based funders including CCHD and the Veatch Program which came together in 1998 to raise more money for faith-based community organizing. With money

---

[629] www.interfaithfunders.org/aboutus.html

[630] As of August 2010, there were 12 members: The Evangelical Lutheran Church In America's Division for Church in Society, One Great Hour of Sharing Fund of the Presbyterian Church (U.S.A.), Catholic Campaign for Human Development, Unitarian Universalist Veatch Program at Shelter Rock, Jewish Funds for Justice, The McKnight Foundation, The Nathan Cummings Foundation, Dominican Sisters of Springfield, Missionary Oblates of Mary Immaculate, C.S. Mott Foundation, The Needmor Fund, Linchpin Project of the Center for Community Change, and Unitarian Universalist Funding Panels. www.interfaithfunders.org/aboutus.html

from the consortium members and from the Ford
and Surdna foundations, Interfaith Funders gave
nearly $1 million in grants during 1998 and
1999.[631]

Some of these grants go towards research projects supportive
of congregation-based community organizing and to "provide
workshops on CBCO at funder
conferences and briefings, and gatherings of faith communities,
as well as individual
meetings. IF also offers members valuable networking and
internal education."[632]

IF is concerned to see that the Alinskyian community
organizing networks prosper. A forthcoming project (at the
time of this writing) of IF is a study, "Congregation-Based
Community Organizing: State of the Field 2010-11." According
to Ned Wight, IF's board president and the Executive Director
of the Unitarian Universalist Veatch Program at Shelter Rock,
"We are keenly aware that community organizing has evolved a
great deal since 2000. Our goal for the State of the Field 2010-
11 project is to discern how the field has evolved, and what new
challenges and opportunities it now faces, in order to fund the
field more strategically."[633]

To facilitate networking among organizers, Interfaith
Funders launched the Inter-Religious Organizing Initiative (IOI)
in 2002, when ELCA Presiding Bishop Mark Hanson and Dr.

---

[631] Robert O. Bothwell, "Research Analysis - What are the Alternatives,"
Council on Foundations, *Foundations News and Commentary*, May/June 2002
[632] www.interfaithfunders.org/aboutus.html
[633] Interfaith Funders Press release, "New Study Being Launched:
Congregation-Based Community Organizing: State of the Field 2010-11," 12-
1-10.

William Shaw, President of the National Baptist Convention USA "convened a meeting of their peers from several national faith bodies. They discussed cooperative civic action according to the principles of congregation-based organizing. The result was the commissioning of the "IOI Table."[634] Faith leaders at "the Table" commit to involving their congregations more deeply in public life and to developing national power building processes.[635]

The IOI Table includes not only Interfaith Funders' members but also representatives from the primary Alinskyian organizing networks – Gamaliel Foundation, DART (Direct Action and Research Training), and PICO (People's Institute for Community Organizing), and Interfaith Worker Justice, as well as Faith in Public Life.[636]

Susan Leslie, UUA Director of the Office for Congregational Advocacy and Witness, explains the attraction of the IOI Table:

> Like other religious associations, we have congregations engaged in CBCO [congregation-based community organizing] with all the major networks, as well as some regional ones. It's to our benefit to gather with other religious associations who are in the same situation to examine the gains and the challenges of

---

[634] www.elca.org/Our-Faith-In-Action/Justice/Congregation-based-Organizing/Enewsletter.aspx#4

[635] Inter-Religious Organizing Initiative (IOI) Working Table, "A Statement of the IOI Planning Team," revised August 1, 2007. The Planning Team members included: Terry Boggs, ELCA; Dennis Jacobsen, ELCA; Charles Mock, National Baptist Convention, USA, Inc.; Cris Doby, Charles Stewart Mott Foundation; Len Dubi, Archdiocese of Chicago; and Kathy Partridge, Interfaith Funders.

[636] "UUA Joins Interfaith Organizing Initiative at Historic Gathering in Nashville," News, 12-19-07; "A Statement of the IOI Planning Team…" also mentions The Center for Community Change (CCC).

congregation-based community organizing and to work together to share these lessons with the organizing networks. An exciting prospect is to work toward gathering national strength. Bringing the interfaith community, the organizing networks, and the funders together at one table has allowed us to increase the impact of CBCO exponentially.[637]

Specifically, the IOI sees congregation-based community organizing "as a vehicle for training clergy and lay leadership at the congregational level, for deepening the capacities of our denominations and religious bodies powerfully and faithfully to enter the national public arena for the sake of justice, and for increasing the capacity of our voice in the national public arena."[638]

Specific "justice issues" are selected as appropriate for engagement at the national level — issues selected from among "those which arise out of the grassroots organizing efforts of participating networks, which converge with the interests of participating denominations and religious bodies...," drawing on "media and communications consultants, theologians, denominational advocacy offices, political analysts, and experts in message framing" to shape "its public voice and national strategy."[639]

SECULAR FUNDERS

---

[637] "UUA Joins Interfaith Organizing ..."
[638] "A Statement of the IOI Planning Team..."
[639] "A Statement of the IOI Planning Team..."

The above has focused on the funding provided by religious bodies to promote the faith-based, Alinskyian organizing networks. Secular bodies are deeply invested in this, as well.

Page 14 of the 2009 Annual Report for the Gamaliel Foundation lists its organizational contributors.[640] Some of them are what one would expect, such as the Presbyterian Church USA (in other words, religious bodies) and the Ford and Rockefeller Foundations who have been funding faith-based organizing for years.[641]

Others are less expected – for example, the Service Employees International Union (SEIU). Faith in Public Life is another curious contributor. This organization describes itself as a "strategy center advancing faith in the public square as a positive and unifying force for justice, compassion and the common good."[642] Funding an Alinskyian organizing network, in other words, is a Faith in Public Life strategy to advance its vision of justice. The contribution to Gamaliel's work "buys" a stake in Gamaliel's efforts among faith institutions to spread the "vision" – which defines "justice" in progressive, political terms.

Another particularly interesting contributor to the Gamaliel Foundation is the Center for Community Change (CCC). CCC was created to provide technical assistance to various local community organizations but, under the leadership of former ACORN organizer Deepak Bhargava, has become a "political machine," coordinating local organizations such as Gamaliel affiliates, which are CCC "partners," in national campaigns.

The next question is where do Faith in Public Life and the Center for Community Change get the money to give to Gamaliel? Among *their* contributors is George Soros' Open

---

[640] www.gamaliel.org/Portals/0/Documents/
Gamaliel2009AnnualReport.pdf
[641] *The Coercive Utopians* (1985) details this funding source.
[642] faithinpubliclife.org/about

Society Institute.[643] Faith in Public Life received two $225,000 grants from Open Society Institute in 2009-2010. For its part, CCC received two Open Society Institute grants in 2008: $600,000 for "general support" and another $250,000 specifically for its Immigration Reform Movement efforts; in 2009, it received an additional $930,000. That's not exactly chump change…and one can see how Faith in Public Life and CCC might have a bit left over to pass along to Gamaliel.

Of course, Gamaliel has been getting its own grants directly from the Open Society Institute - $300,000 over two years in 2008 and a second award of $300,000 beginning in 2010. The Open Society Institute, in other words, is another institutional contributor to Gamaliel, directly and, one might argue, indirectly.

George Soros' Open Society Institute's funding of Gamaliel - or, for that matter, Faith in Public Life, CCC, and the other Alinskyian organizing networks [644] – is an investment in progressive values. Open Society Institute has generously funded Catholics for a Free Choice, Planned Parenthood, the

---

[643] All Open Society Institute grants cited here can be found at the OSI website, grantee listings:
www.soros.org/initiatives/usprograms/focus/democracy/grants/civic/gran tees?sort_on=sort_title&sort_desc=0&start:int=0

[644] Open Society Institute funded the Industrial Areas Foundation network through its "organizing, technical assistance, training, and research" component, the Interfaith Education Fund, which received an 18-month grant for $300,000 in 2008 and another 1-year grant for $200,000 in 2010. The PICO network received a 2-year Open Society Institute grant for $600,000 in 2009. National Training and Information Center received a 2009 Open Society Institute grant for $600,000 over a 2-year period. Catholics in Alliance for the Common Good (the now defunct twin of Faith in Public Life's Catholics United) received $50,000 in 2005, $100,000 in 2006, and another $100,000 in 2009 from the Open Society Institute. [See *Anne Hendershott, "Who are these Fake Catholic Groups," The Catholic Advocate, 3-18-10]*

National Abortion Rights Action League (NARAL), and a host of other abortion "rights" organizations. It has funded the United Religions Initiative (URI), which promulgates the idea that all religions and spiritual movements are equally "true" and with it the concept that the goal of the spiritual is social reform – including the principle of population control.[645] The faith-based Alinskyian organizing networks are right there, working "for change" among Catholics and Evangelicals and other religious bodies that might, historically, have been expected to resist progressive positions such as these.

---

[645] See Lee Penn, *False Dawn: The United Religions Initiative, Globalism, and the Quest for a One-World Religion*, Sophia Perennis, 2004.

Jack Egan

Cesar Chavez

Made in the USA
San Bernardino, CA
30 September 2014